# The Logic of Commitment

T0299972

"A brief but compelling study of the logic and morality of personal commitments, and their importance for a life well lived. Gary Chartier's clear prose and wide reading make this an important contribution to ethical and meta-ethical theory."

**—Stephen R. L. Clark**, University of Liverpool

"'Commitments matter,' writes Gary Chartier in his new book: 'they provide needed structure and direction for our lives . . . and the grounding we need to craft stable identities and secure our projects.' In this careful, scholarly, and revealing study Chartier develops a conception of commitments that shows their deep analogy with promises, and makes important headway on some of the puzzles and problems that the notion of a commitment raises for our theory of motivation and practical reason. This book can be recommended to anyone who wants to see how a distinctively non-consequentialist philosophical ethics can be put together on the basis of a deep pluralism about the human goods."

**—Sophie-Grace Chappell**, Open University

"In this engaging and original discussion of commitment, Gary Chartier distinguishes commitments from promises, and shows the role commitments play in love, in creating and sustaining an integrated self, in character development, and in well-being. A commitment is a firm resolve to do or be something that binds the agent's future actions and attitudes; it may involve others, but it is an obligation to oneself, not to others. For example, one can make a commitment to keep a promise to someone. This generates self-regarding reasons, in addition to the obvious other-regarding ones, for keeping the promise. This concern for the self one creates and preserves through one's commitments is very much in the spirit of a natural law or eudaimonistic ethics, showing the value of making commitments serves to provide further support for this ethics."

**—Neera Badhwar**, University of Oklahoma

This book develops and defends a conception of commitment and explores its limits. Gary Chartier shows how commitment serves to resolve conflicts between ordinary moral intuitions and the reality that the basic aspects of human well-being are incommensurable. He outlines a variety of overlapping and mutually reinforcing rationales for making commitments, explores the relationship between commitment and vocation and the relevance of commitment to love, and notes some reasons why it might make sense to disregard one's commitments. *The Logic of Commitment* will appeal to ethicists interested in the connection between commitment and personal well-being, and to anyone who wonders why and when it might make sense to make or keep commitments.

**Gary Chartier** is Distinguished Professor of Law and Business Ethics at La Sierra University.

# Routledge Focus on Philosophy

*Routledge Focus on Philosophy* is an exciting and innovative new series, capturing and disseminating some of the best and most exciting new research in philosophy in short book form. Peer reviewed and at a maximum of fifty thousand words shorter than the typical research monograph, *Routledge Focus on Philosophy* titles are available in both ebook and print on demand format. Tackling big topics in a digestible format, the series opens up important philosophical research for a wider audience, and as such is invaluable reading for the scholar, researcher and student seeking to keep their finger on the pulse of the discipline. The series also reflects the growing interdisciplinarity within philosophy and will be of interest to those in related disciplines across the humanities and social sciences.

**Forthcoming titles:**

**The Logic of Commitment**
*Gary Chartier*

**Plant Minds**
*Chauncey Maher*

**Moral Thinking: Fast and Slow**
*Hanno Sauer*

**Knowledge Transmission**
*Stephen Wright*

**Mind-reading and the Philosophy of Social Cognition**
*Shannon Spaulding*

www.routledge.com/Routledge-Focus-on-Philosophy/book-series/RFP

# The Logic of Commitment

**Gary Chartier**

Routledge
Taylor & Francis Group

LONDON AND NEW YORK

First published 2018
by Routledge

2 Park Square, Milton Park, Abingdon, Oxfordshire OX14 4RN
52 Vanderbilt Avenue, New York, NY 10017

*Routledge is an imprint of the Taylor & Francis Group, an informa business*

First issued in paperback 2020

Copyright © 2018 Taylor & Francis

*Library of Congress Cataloging-in-Publication Data*
A catalog record for this book has been requested

ISBN: 978-1-138-30148-1 (hbk)
ISBN: 978-0-367-60734-0 (pbk)

Typeset in Times New Roman
by Apex CoVantage, LLC

*For you,*
*at the water fountain*
*in front of the white horse*

# Contents

# Acknowledgments

Thanks as always to the usual suspects—A. Ligia Radoias, Aena Prakash, Annette Bryson, Alexander Lian, Andrew Howe, Carole Pateman, Christopher C. Reeves, Craig R. Kinzer, David B. Hoppe, David Gordon, David R. Larson, Deborah K. Dunn, Donna L. Carlson, Eddy Palacios, Elenor L. Webb, Ellen Hubbell, Eva Pascal, Jeffrey D. Cassidy, Joel Wilson, John Thomas, Julio C. Muñoz, Kenneth A. Dickey, Ladan Ask, Lawrence T. Geraty, Linn Marie Tonstad, Maria Zlateva, Melissa Cushman, Michael Orlando, Nabil Abu-Assal, Patricia M. Cabrera, Roger E. Rustad, Jr., Ronel S. Harvey, Ruth E. E. Burke, Sel J. Hwahng, Sheldon Richman, Tanja M. Laden, Trisha Famisaran, W. Kent Rogers, and Wonil Kim—for the usual reasons.

Brian Hebblethwaite, John Hick, Michael Banner, Seana Shiffrin, Stephen R. L. Clark, and Stephen R. Munzer all played valuable roles at various points in my post-baccalaureate formation as a philosopher; none of them should, of course, be held responsible for what I've written here. A number of philosophers—notably Bernard Williams, David Schmidtz, Germain Grisez, John Finnis, Jon Elster, Joseph Raz, Margaret Farley, Mark C. Murphy, Robert P. George, and Robert Nozick—have taught me much of what I know of a theoretical nature about commitment, and I have drawn shamelessly, even if with acknowledgment, on their many valuable insights and formulations. At the same time, commitment is a topic probably explored at least as much outside as within the academy, and much of what I've learned about commitment, its consequences, and what's needed to safeguard it I've learned from writers—often coaches, counselors, or therapists—whose names might not ordinarily turn up in philosophical footnotes. They include Barbara De Angelis, Blase Harris, Clay Andrews and Mika Terao, David Truman, Elaine Claire von Keudell, Gayle and Hugh Prather, Harville Hendrix and Helen LaKelly Hunt, Henry Cloud and John Townsend, John Gottman, Judith Sills, Linda and Charlie Bloom, Shmuley Boteach, and Thomas W. McKnight.

David Gordon has demonstrated the authentic commitment of a true friend in the course of carefully reviewing this book in advance of its publication—with respect to some portions, on multiple occasions. With characteristic rapidity and insight, Sandy Thatcher offered useful advice regarding both the publication process and the book's content. Various anonymous readers also provided thoughtful comments for which I'm certainly appreciative. And I have every reason to be thankful as well to Tanja Laden, Stephen R. L. Clark, Alexander Lian, Coco Owen, Sophia Assal, and others for conversations about the book as it developed, and to Neera Badhwar for helpfully noting the need for a variety of corrections.

La Sierra University served as the context for my research and writing. John Thomas, Randal Wisbey, Joy Fehr, and Cheryl Bauman all deserve thanks for enabling me to work on this book during my time at La Sierra. Libraries play an indispensable role in all research, obviously, and mine has been no exception. So I am happy as always to express my gratitude for the assistance given me by members of the La Sierra University Library's faculty and staff, including Hilda Smith, Jeff de Vries, Jill Start, Kitty Simmons, Sandra Hartson, and others.

I owe an obvious debt of gratitude to Andrew Weckenmann at Routledge for his support for this book, and to Fiona Hudson, Dana Richards, Denise File, and Katie McIlvanie for facilitating the rapid production of the book, ensuring its æsthetic appeal, and helping to make my writing clearer and more accurate. I also acknowledge with great appreciation the willingness of Sophie-Grace Chappell, Stephen R. L. Clark, and Neera Badhwar to craft endorsements for the book.

As usual, I will donate the author royalties I receive for this book to Anti-War.com. I am grateful to this exceptional source of news and inspirer of activism for its role in fostering peace, and freedom. I encourage all of my readers to consider supporting it.

While it has been in various ways reorganized and rewritten, I have drawn here on some previously published work.[1] I'm thankful for the permission I've received to use it here.

## Note

1 The relevant texts: Gary Chartier, *Left-Wing Market Anarchism and Natural Law*, 7 STUD. EMERGENT ORD. 314 (2014); Gary Chartier, *Incommensurable Basic Goods*, 40 AUSTL. J. LEGAL PHIL. 1 (2015); GARY CHARTIER, ECONOMIC JUSTICE AND NATURAL LAW 61–64 (2009).

# Introduction
## Exploring Commitment

*There are various, mutually reinforcing reasons to make and keep commitments, which help to structure and support our flourishing.*

A *commitment* as I understand it is a resolution, a plan, a decision, a choice that is treated by the person making it as not to be altered simply at will. (If the person making it feels free to alter it at will, perhaps it's better seen as an *intention*.) A commitment in this sense serves to render some previously unsettled aspect of one's future determinate. A commitment may be conscious and deliberate, but it need not be, perhaps because it engages the will as a matter of habit or affective attachment or because it is consciously ratified only after it has become habitual. Some examples of what I mean by *commitment* include:

- I decide that I won't answer the phone this morning in order to enable myself to get some work done.
- I commit to writing a work-related report before going out this evening.
- I elect to give up alcohol for the next month.
- I resolve to train for a half-marathon during the remainder of the year.
- I plan to take up performing with a local band as a hobby.
- I opt to accept someone as a friend.
- I choose to become a physician.
- I decide to move to Cleveland.

I make a commitment at least in part to ensure that I don't encounter each choice *de novo*: I don't begin by considering what to do in the future without regard to my past commitment. (Otherwise, I would have no reason to make a *commitment*—I would simply form intentions that were always capable of being revised. To make a commitment just is to choose to constrain one's future options in a way not subject to alteration at will.) Commitments are defensible in a variety of distinct but mutually reinforcing ways. They should be taken seriously, even as we may sometimes have reason to revise or abandon them.

A commitment may be limited in extent and may feature a variety of built-in escape clauses: I commit myself, say, to exercising by three o'clock this afternoon even if, at three, I don't feel any enthusiasm at the prospect of exercise. I've ruled out lack of enthusiasm as a reason for not exercising, but I may not have ruled out, and may, indeed, have explicitly allowed for, the possibility of abandoning my exercise plans if my partner proposes that we go out sooner than I'd anticipated, or if an out-of-town visitor arrives, or if I've managed to muster more momentum for a writing project than I'd expected I would. A commitment, that is, excludes some potential reasons for non-fulfillment, but it need not exclude many others.

Alternatively, of course, a commitment may be thoroughly open-ended, and it may preclude almost all reasons for non-fulfillment: I may commit myself, say, to rescuing the imprisoned Richard the Lionhearted—and to investing as much time and money in this project as may be needed to bring it to fruition, and to continue trying to liberate the king until I either succeed or die in the process. A commitment need not exclude many reasons for non-fulfillment, but it may perfectly well do so.

Whether it's carefully delimited or thoroughly open-ended, what is distinctive about a commitment understood this way is that it involves my assumption of an obligation *on my own* (even if in various ways it may affect others, too, and may be intended to do so). A commitment-based obligation isn't an obligation *to* anyone else. But this doesn't mean that ignoring it at will would be reasonable or that I am entitled to dispense myself of it whenever I want to do so.

Because they're not made to others, commitments are distinct from promises, though they help to organize our lives in not dissimilar ways. If promises are, as I take them to be, obligatory in virtue of others' trust or reliance,[1] the reasons for keeping a commitment, presuming there are any, will be different from, even if they in one way or another resemble, the reasons for keeping a promise. Serious promises—especially ones that rule out many reasons for non-fulfillment and are relatively open-ended—are sometimes referred to as "commitments."[2] But, when I talk about commitments, I mean specifically to denote serious decisions made by oneself, decisions that do not as such involve *interpersonal* obligations. Commitments may concern others, be undertaken in the interests of others; but they are not made *to* others.

It is perfectly possible, of course, that I might *promise* you that I will do something, and so assume a promissory obligation to you, while simultaneously making a *commitment* to doing the same thing, and so generating further, independent reasons in virtue of which non-performance would be inappropriate. I might subsequently find that I was no longer obligated to keep the promise even though I was still required to fulfill the commitment; or I might find that the commitment no longer bound me even as the promise did.

A common contemporary division within ethics, a division between morality and prudence, often disposes us to treat some aspects of morality, at least, as binding always and everywhere, while viewing prudence as more or less optional. But of course ethics as classically conceived drew no sharp distinction between morality and prudence—or, indeed, between a concern with the self and a concern with the other. Exploring the idea of commitment is perhaps one way of getting at what an approach to ethics of a more classical sort might look like and why it might appeal. Thus, my goal here is to illuminate what an approach to ethics by way of flourishing, one in accordance with which reasoning about self and other proceeds in the same way and in light of the same considerations, might look like in practice.

I am particularly interested in one such approach—the New Classical Natural Law (NCNL) theory, which deliberately focuses on flourishing and integrates concern for self and concern for the other.[3] I won't seek to expound or defend this view here in general, though a number of the things I say in, for instance, Chapter 3 are certainly germane to a vindication of the theory. But I will draw on or presuppose my own, non-standard version at various points. Roughly, this theory holds that there are various aspects of flourishing, well-being, welfare, or fulfillment—"basic goods." Something like the following is arguably a reasonably comprehensive list of the various aspects of flourishing: life and bodily well-being, knowledge, practical reasonableness, play, skillful performance, friendship and sociability, æsthetic experience, imaginative immersion, meaning and harmony with reality in the widest sense, sensory pleasure,[4] and self-integration and inner peace. These dimensions of fulfillment are real—not simply reducible to our reactions or responses to them—and incommensurable, and individual instances of each are non-fungible.[5] A choice with respect to flourishing is reasonable to the extent that it (*i*) intends to realize, promote, or respect a genuine aspect of well-being (the Principle of Recognition); (*ii*) does not arbitrarily discriminate among those affected (the Principle of Fairness); (*iii*) seeks to realize, promote, or respect a given aspect of well-being at the least cost possible given the goal of realizing, promoting, or respecting that aspect of well-being (the Principle of Efficiency); (*iv*) does not involve purposeful or instrumental injury to any aspect of well-being (the Principle of Respect); and (*v*) involves reasonable regard for the chooser's commitments (the Principle of Commitment).[6] The various principles interact with and support each other: what is fair in a given case may be constrained by one's prior commitments; one may not assume a commitment-grounded obligation to mount a purposeful attack on some aspect of well-being (by, say, becoming a public executioner); and so forth.

I am concerned here with an issue that arises particularly in connection with approaches, like NCNL theory, that embrace incommensurability: I will seek to show why commitments are crucial in light of the reality that the options we confront embody incommensurable goods. But this book is not an exercise in natural law theory. Nor is it, more generally, intended primarily as an exposition of the kind of theoretical stance I'd like to defend. Rather, I've written it because I believe that commitments *matter*, that they provide needed structure and direction for our lives while allowing us to fashion with relative freedom the trajectories along which we will proceed. They provide us with the grounding we need to craft stable identities that are distinctively our own, and they help to secure projects that matter to us against the effects of the fluctuations in feeling that beset all of us.

Commitments can help us achieve our goals both causally and normatively. Sometimes, a commitment will yield significant reasons for action and judgment because of the causal consequences of making the commitment: in virtue of my self-investment or of circumstantial factors I have anticipated or helped to create or both, I can (*i*) habituate myself in such a way that I'm disposed to behave in a given manner or (*ii*) alter the incentives to which I'm responding in ways likely to affect my behavior. And sometimes I may judge that, whatever my emotional inclination, just because I've already made a decision to commit, it's now unreasonable for me to disregard my commitment even when I am inclined to do so. *Ex ante*, commitments and the subsidiary choices that implement or support them can contribute directly or indirectly to shaping preferences and dispositions that influence our subsequent choices. *Ex post*, commitments can constitute or generate reasons for action that it would be inappropriate for us to ignore.

In what follows, I consider and, where necessary, reconstruct a variety of complementary, overlapping rationales for making and keeping commitments, seeking to explain why each is or isn't a source of reasons we ought to embrace. I explain how commitments resemble but also differ from vocations, which might be thought to play similar moral and existential roles. And I illustrate my approach to commitment by explaining how it might play out in the context of love.

I begin, in Chapter 1, by exploring the role of commitments on a purely instrumental conception of rationality, since whatever can be defended on such a conception will also be relevant on other, more robust conceptions of reason. I examine what would be required for someone to care about the future or the past at all on an instrumental conception of reason before going on to consider several functions commitments might play on such a conception. Keeping self-determining commitments helps us to master ourselves, and so to become people we and others can rely on more readily in relation not only to these commitments (if reliance is an issue) but also in relation to other commitments more generally. In addition, keeping such commitments can be a genuine challenge; doing so can thus enable us to earn our own respect. And substantive commitments mean we will have reasons to continue living and choosing and acting—reasons we might wish on instrumental grounds to have.

Keeping commitments is a matter of rendering ourselves coherent, I suggest in Chapter 2, a matter of making *our stories* coherent, of crafting a stable identity, and of safeguarding the identities we have already formed. It is also a matter of achieving coherence between our acts of planning or committing or resolving on the one hand and our subsequent choices on the other.

Commitments serve to structure our lives in light of the inescapable need to choose among incommensurable, non-fungible goods. Thus, I begin Chapter 3 by examining and defending the notion of such goods. The basic aspects of human well-being are incommensurable and non-fungible. There are good, positive reasons to take this to be the case, and challenges to the idea of incommensurability don't succeed. Because these aspects of well-being are incommensurable, planning and cost-benefit analysis beyond the immediate moment make sense only in light of commitments that establish personal and institutional priorities. We must have hierarchies of goods in order to plan, and these hierarchies must be established by our commitments. In addition, commitment serves to resolve conflicts between ordinary moral intuitions and the idea of incommensurability. And commitments make possible kinds and degrees of participation in various kinds of well-being that would otherwise be difficult or impossible.

The idea of commitment seems to play a role not dissimilar to that of vocation, insofar as it involves making particular tasks and goods central to an agent's identity. While morality in general leaves us with many options, commitments and vocations alike seem to make particular paths distinctively our own. Vocations seem to be given to us (in the focal instance in Western thought, by divine commands), while commitments are chosen. But, I argue in Chapter 4, the distinction may not be as pronounced as it first appears to be.

In Chapter 5, I illustrate the significance of my approach to commitment by considering its relevance to erotic love. A commitment or set of commitments with regard to a love-relationship should be distinguished from promises made in the context of such a relationship. Such a commitment or set of commitments can enable us to continue engaging long enough to reach deep and persistent intimacy, to evoke responsive commitments (and love), to give and keep giving to the beloved, and to offer the beloved security. Being committed to caring for and being with another can also offer the giver the opportunity to safeguard a valued relationship in the face of fickle feeling.

I emphasize in the Conclusion that we have good reason to make commitments. Doing so is first and foremost an aspect of our own flourishing or fulfillment rather than an interpersonal obligation. But it doesn't make sense to think of making commitments if we don't keep them. At the same time, the inner logic of commitment helps to provide a variety of reasons why particular commitments or plans might reasonably be revised or abandoned.

## Notes

1  For what strike me as useful accounts of promissory obligation, *see, e.g.*, T. M. SCANLON, WHAT WE OWE TO EACH OTHER 295–327 (1998); JOHN FINNIS, NATURAL LAW AND NATURAL RIGHTS 298–314 (1980). I believe Scanlon is correct that an *institution* of promising isn't needed for individual instances of promising and promise-keeping to make sense and for individual promissory obligations to obtain.

2  Commitments understood as serious promises are very much in focus in MARGARET A. FARLEY, PERSONAL COMMITMENTS (1986)—an excellent book indeed and certainly attentive to the ways in which people use the language of commitment. Similarly, Allan Farnsworth employs "commitment" to mean "a voluntary undertaking to do something in the *future*"—an undertaking to someone else, and so what I would label a "promise": E. ALLAN FARNSWORTH, CHANGING YOUR MIND: THE LAW OF REGRETTED DECISIONS 3 (1998). Sandy Thatcher notes that agreements by high school athletes to accept offers of places on American college football teams are characteristically referred to as commitments as well. I have no burden to argue that everyone does or should use the word "commitment" the way I do here. I take myself, though, to have focused on a central meaning of the word; and using a familiar term seems preferable to concocting a term of art likely to prove not only unfamiliar but also lacking emotional resonance.

3  *See, e.g.*, FINNIS, LAW, *supra* note 1; JOHN FINNIS, FUNDAMENTALS OF ETHICS (1983); 1 GERMAIN GRISEZ, THE WAY OF THE LORD JESUS: CHRISTIAN MORAL PRINCIPLES (1983); GERMAIN GRISEZ & RUSSELL SHAW, BEYOND THE NEW MORALITY: THE RESPONSIBILITIES OF FREEDOM (3d ed. 1988); JOHN M. FINNIS ET AL., NUCLEAR DETERRENCE, MORALITY, AND REALISM (1987); GERMAIN GRISEZ & JOSEPH M. BOYLE, JR., LIFE AND DEATH WITH LIBERTY AND JUSTICE: A CONTRIBUTION TO THE EUTHANASIA DEBATE (1979); JOHN FINNIS, MORAL ABSOLUTES: TRADITION, REVISION, AND TRUTH (1991); 2 GERMAIN G. GRISEZ, THE WAY OF THE LORD JESUS: LIVING A CHRISTIAN LIFE (1994); JOHN FINNIS, AQUINAS: MORAL, POLITICAL, AND LEGAL THEORY (1998); ROBERT P. GEORGE, IN DEFENSE OF NATURAL LAW (2001); 3 GERMAIN GRISEZ, THE WAY OF THE LORD JESUS: DIFFICULT MORAL QUESTIONS (1997); Germain Grisez et al., *Practical Principles, Moral Truth, and Ultimate Ends*, 32 AM. J. JURIS 99 (1987); John M. Finnis et al., *"Direct" and "Indirect": A Reply to Critics of Our Action Theory*, 65 THOMIST 1 (2001). *Cf.* MARK C. MURPHY, NATURAL LAW AND PRACTICAL RATIONALITY (1999); MARK C. MURPHY, NATURAL LAW IN JURISPRUDENCE AND POLITICS (2006); ALFONSO GÓMEZ-LOBO, MORALITY AND THE HUMAN GOODS: AN INTRODUCTION TO NATURAL LAW ETHICS (2002); TIMOTHY CHAPPELL, UNDERSTANDING HUMAN GOODS: A THEORY OF ETHICS (1995).

4  *See, e.g.,* CHAPPELL, *supra* note 3; THOMAS NAGEL, THE VIEW FROM NOWHERE 156–
62 (1986). Standard NCNL theory rejects the notion that sensory pleasure is a
basic good.

5  *See, e.g.,* CHAPPELL, *supra* note 3, at 37–45; MURPHY, RATIONALITY, *supra* note 3,
at 96–138; GÓMEZ-LOBO, *supra* note 3, at 6–25; GRISEZ & SHAW, *supra* note 3, at
77–88; GRISEZ, PRINCIPLES, *supra* note 3, at 121–25; FINNIS, LAW, *supra* note 1, at
59–99.

6  *See, e.g.,* GRISEZ & SHAW, *supra* note 3, at 117–53; GRISEZ, PRINCIPLES, *supra* note
3, at 205–28; FINNIS, LAW, *supra* note 1, at 100–33; FINNIS, ETHICS, *supra* note 3, at
75–76; MURPHY, RATIONALITY, *supra* note 3, at 198–212; GÓMEZ-LOBO, *supra* note
3, at 42–44. The specific list and the labels are my own.

# 1 Commitment and Instrumental Reason

*Making and keeping commitments can help us realize our preferences—by encouraging our subsequent pursuit of particular goals, changing our assessments of contrary preferences, helping us develop valuable character traits, and evoking positive responses from others.*

## I. Commitments Help Us Achieve a Broad Range of Goals

Making and keeping commitments makes sense strategically or instrumentally. In Part II, I reflect on the general question of how thinking about the future and the past can make sense when we're reasoning instrumentally. In Part III, I examine specific links between commitment-keeping and instrumental rationality. I sum up in Part IV.

## II. Thinking Instrumentally Outside the Present

Rightly or wrongly, instrumental reason is often thought to be the simplest and most transparent variety of reason.[1] It is concerned straightforwardly with achieving one's goals in as inexpensive a manner as possible. Making sense of commitment in this context requires some sense of our identity over time and of our entitlement to speak for our future selves.

### A. *Making and Keeping Commitments Presupposes Identity over Time*

Whether making and keeping commitments is instrumentally rational depends in part on whether one's identity is meaningfully preserved over time, on whether the self making the commitment and the self wondering whether to honor the commitment are in important respects the same. Sorting out the challenge of keeping commitments need not involve exploring complex cases about (full or partial) brain-switching, resurrections, disembodiment, and the like. A fairly straightforward and simple understanding of personal identity as narrative continuity will do.[2] I need enough of a sense of personal identity over time that it makes sense for me to hold myself responsible for past choices (as, of course, for others to hold me responsible for these choices as well in appropriate circumstances) and to constrain future choices. If I can hold myself responsible for past choices, then it seems as if I can *make* choices for which I can expect myself to accept responsibility in the future and so, when they are intended to shape the future direction of my actions, to adhere to them.

To the challenge that I can reinvent myself on a moment-by-moment basis, and so needn't regard my present self as identical with my past self in a way that imposes any obligations on me, I might consider a multifold response, quite apart from the intricate metaphysical issues involved.[3] (*i*) Reasoning in this way would be inconsistent with choosing rationally and planning for the future. The practice of planning for the future presupposes continuity of identity. (*ii*) Reasoning in this way is inconsistent with our actual practices of holding ourselves and others responsible. (*iii*) Reasoning in this way would make social life of various sorts impossible. While hardly decisive, these considerations at least suggest how disruptive of individual lives and social institutions were we to abandon the practice of treating ourselves as persisting over time.

## B.  *Speaking for My Future Self*

One might wonder what entitles me to tie my own future hands. (*i*) Perhaps there is some reason to be suspicious that the later influence one seeks in the present to blunt will be worth rejecting. There may be multiple justifications for this stance, but the most obvious is that the influence interferes with the capacity for rational choice itself, with a capacity that is essential if an agent is to pursue and achieve (almost) any goal imaginable (allowing for the cases in which rational choice actually conflicts with the achievement of one's goals). So, in the interest of achieving all of one's other goals, one might reasonably tie one's hands, literally or figuratively.

(*ii*) In many cases, though, the future contingencies I want to preclude by committing now won't involve any interference with the capacity for rational choice. Consider the training regimen to which I might commit in order to prepare for a half-marathon. What's likely to impede it is not some sort of rationality-stultifying plague, but simply the physical tiredness associated with persistent training, the boredom that accompanies it, the thought that I have no chance of doing well in the final contest in any case. None of these is a disposition that simply eliminates rationality. Instrumental rationality serves simply to help us achieve our goals. And the coming-to-preeminence of one of the negative motives to which I've alluded here would simply mean that I had come to embrace a goal different from the one that had previously claimed my loyalty.

Of course, I can't avoid making choices that will affect my future self. Any choice I make in the present will causally influence my future circumstances in various ways. In addition, my present choices can be expected to reshape my future preferences. It makes no sense to treat those future preferences as formed in pristine fashion, independent of what I'm doing in the present. Non-interference with my future self isn't realistically *possible*.

At the same time, the issue of commitment arises precisely because our preferences frequently conflict. Accepting the goal to which I'm committed in the face of contrary current preferences will mean treating my commitment as decisive. It will mean forming and acting on preferences shaped by my commitment. And it will mean grounding my resistance to my current preferences for another option or options in the preferences shaped by my commitment. Keeping the commitment will need to be, in one way or another, the most efficient way of achieving one's goals.

## C. Instrumental Reason and Commitment

Instrumental rationality is essentially forward-looking, though of course it can feature various derivative reasons for attending to the past. But a commitment is a past event. The point of a commitment might be thought to be precisely to constrain one's future choices when one might *prefer* to do something other than whatever it is to which one is committed. A commitment need not be counter-preferential, since one might well prefer at many or all points in the future to do whatever one has committed oneself to doing. But a commitment will obviously matter, particularly when one desires strongly to abandon the plan embodied in the commitment. The point of the commitment will be to interpose itself between reaction and choice, so that one will *not*, in fact, act on one's preference to abandon the pursuit of one's goal.

It might seem, then, that a prior commitment could play no independent role in purely instrumental reasoning. *Ex ante*, I may be able to *influence* my future preferences by self-investing emotionally. But why should I care, *ex post*, about a prior commitment? My preferences may change over time. And, if they do, it seems as if, on a model of purely instrumental rationality, I should be concerned with the ones I actually have, not with the ones I wanted to have at some earlier point.

## III. When Making and Keeping Commitments Is Instrumentally Rational

In fact, however, commitments will be relevant to future preferences in at least two ways. I can contribute causally to shaping or reshaping what my preferences actually will be in the future by making a commitment in the present. And I can give myself reason to ignore or discount some future preferences and to attend instead to those embodied in my commitment. In either case, making and keeping commitments is instrumentally rational for at least two broad kinds of reasons. It helps us to achieve specific goals. And it equips us to achieve other, potentially unrelated goals.[4]

## A. *Commitments and Achieving Particular Goals: The* Ex Ante *Perspective*

Some kinds of commitment involve hedging our choices by putting causal constraints on them in place, rather as one might plant booby traps designed to steer someone around the course on which a game is taking place. They may also involve simply investing emotionally in a given project in a way that leads to ongoing pursuit of the project.

Suppose I want to realize a particular preference over an extended period—to continue using the example I've already employed, to train for a half-marathon. I will have reason to make commitments supportive of my goal. As I continue to train for the half-marathon, my desires fluctuate: sometimes I wish to prepare satisfactorily for the half-marathon, while at other times I experience the associated difficulties as overwhelming and tell myself that they are simply "not worth it."

Already aware that this might occur, I can, at the time I embrace a plan to train, also take steps to reduce the risk that I will defect. Perhaps I relocate to a site at which distractions will not be in evidence. Or perhaps I empower someone else to impose a penalty (of a sort on which we agree in advance) on me if I abandon or dilute my training regimen. Thus, to use an example that has become justifiably famous in this context, Odysseus arranges for his associates to tie him to the mast of their ship so that he will not yield to the blandishments of the sirens.[5] At the time he asks to be bound, he knows that his later self will prove all too responsive to the sirens' songs; wishing to prevent this, he ensures that his own hands are tied before he can be seduced. Perhaps in my own case I make a bet with a friend, agreeing to pay a painfully large sum if I don't qualify for the marathon. Given my goal of participating, imposing the risk of a penalty on myself in this way can be a rational means of achieving my goal.

But the primary form making a commitment will likely take on the spare view of instrumental rationality I am considering here will be to form habits.[6] That is, making a commitment will mean contributing causally in various ways to the formation of the disposition to adhere to whatever plan is embodied in the commitment. That fact that I make a commitment now will matter at some later time when I am disposed to ignore the commitment precisely because I will have made myself into the kind of person who will keep the commitment anyway. "Until one is committed," W. H. Murray observes in *The Scottish Himalayan Expedition*, "there is hesitancy, the chance to draw back, always ineffectiveness."[7] But in committing, one invests oneself—and pushes oneself forward.

Of course, once a commitment is made, it will become easier to keep not only because keeping it will become a habit but also because having made and begun to keep it will shape one's preferences in such a way that keeping it will be an increasingly natural expression of those preferences, with the result that one will *feel* good about the achievement of one's goals because of one's commitment to achieving them and because, since one has organized one's life in relation to the commitment, there will be an increasingly smooth *fit* between keeping the commitment and the other choices one makes. (Obviously, the focus here is on more extensive commitments. All of this will be less evident, but also less necessary, where short-term commitments—avoiding the phone during a morning of work, say—are concerned.)

The focus here, then, is on my *ex ante* self-cultivation. That I have reason to form the requisite habits does not show that it will on its own be rational to ignore preferences contrary to my commitment when they arise, *ex post*. What it shows, rather, is just that I have reason *ex ante* to develop and solidify preferences supportive of my goal, together with the habit of ignoring or eliminating preferences likely to undermine my commitment-keeping.

## B. Commitments and Achieving Particular Goals: The Ex Post Perspective

Commitment can also operate *without* external restraints and penalties, and even in the absence of felt emotional investment. The committed person may survey the situation she confronts and judge in each moment that she has good reason to keep her commitment even when she feels the urge to avoid doing so. Even in the absence of any extrinsic reward or penalty, she may see reason in virtue of her commitment to behave differently than she would have otherwise. She may, indeed, feel like ignoring the goal to which she is committed or the steps needed to reach that goal. But what's decisive from the perspective of instrumental rationality is her choice, in light of her long-term objective, to adhere to the commitment and so to pursue the goal, to follow the steps.

If one regards one's current preferences as deficient, one may look to a past commitment for motivation. One may be able, let us say, to continue preferring the long-term goal the steps one has committed to making are designed to help one achieve even as one very much would not prefer to perform the individual steps. Psychically, the task of ensuring that the long-term goal continues to enjoy the status it already possesses will be easier if one accords the past commitment some motivational role. *Ex ante*, one will have good reason to encourage the habit of thinking of commitments in this way. But, *ex post*, one may find that, if one sees one's current steps as useful despite their immediate lack of motivational appeal, one may be able to find the needed motivation in a prior commitment.

A further instrumental reason for adhering to a past commitment when habit is insufficient to ensure that one will do so may sometimes be that ongoing adherence to the commitment has resulted in costs of various sorts. Given that one's resource budget is finite, it will often be the case that the likely outcome will involve more preference satisfaction if one continues along the course one has begun than if one starts on another project from scratch. This is only contingently the case, of course; whether, apart from the relevant situational contingencies, we have any reason to give independent weight to sunk costs is another, and more complicated, question to which I will not attend here.[8]

Robert Nozick suggests that, in making a commitment, I am choosing to render it the case that a given instance of compliance or defection symbolizes, stands in for, the entire array of choices complying with or defecting from the commitment.[9] Having chosen in this way, I can't, Nozick says, evaluate an individual decision to abandon my diet just this once with reference only to the costs that decision will itself impose. Instead, once I have made a commitment to go on the diet, any instance of defection will be treated as imposing the costs that abandoning the diet, not just now, but entirely, would lead to my incurring.

Given that I embrace the commitment, I will assess the utility of abandoning the diet in this way. When I make a commitment in the present I am necessarily altering my preferences (perhaps simply by rendering definite what had previously been indefinite): I am assigning fulfillment of the commitment a higher priority than non-fulfillment, and perhaps, indeed, a higher priority than many other states of affairs.

What, however, if my preference with respect to the commitment itself changes, so that I wish to abandon it? It seems, then, that the commitment will no longer be able to confer the needed symbolic significance on any given instance of defection. For a commitment to play the most useful possible role in restraining our responsiveness to temptation, we need to be able to point to the bare fact of having made the commitment as a decisive reason for resisting the temptation even when our other preferences tilt strongly in the contrary direction. Assigning symbolic utility to instances of conformity and defection at the time I make a commitment won't suffice to do this: I will need to *continue* assigning utility in this way. And it seems as if I will need some additional reason to do this apart from simply having made the commitment. (Obviously, if I make a commitment to keep assigning symbolic utility in the needed way, the same problem will arise.)[10]

## C. *Commitments and Achieving General Goals:* Ex Ante *and* Ex Post *Perspectives*

One such additional reason may be the fact that there will be general considerations favoring adherence to commitments *independent* of a particular commitment's role in enabling someone to realize a particular objective. Making and keeping commitments to realize particular goals can at the same time help us achieve other goals.

Adherence to a commitment will make future non-adherence more likely—perhaps not only to the commitment in question but also to commitments in general.[11] The better I am at commitment-keeping in one case, the better I'm likely to be in other cases. And being good at commitment-keeping obviously helps me accomplish my goals. For instance, being reliable, being the sort of person who adheres to her own commitments, facilitates the satisfaction of my preferences because I can more readily make plans that involve long time horizons or in connection with the fulfillment of which I am likely to encounter adversity if I know that I can count on myself to keep these plans.[12] Thus, *ex post*, when confronting a challenge to a commitment or discovering that I have no immediate desire to fulfill the commitment or even to realize the preference the commitment is designed to serve, I will have reason to adhere to the commitment *in order to solidify the general habit of keeping commitments.* This is so, given the ongoing utility to me of not only being believed to have embraced this habit but also of *actually* having embraced it.

Commitments also protect us against acting impulsively.[13] If we understand that our long-term preference-satisfaction will be served when we don't always give in to impulse, a commitment can serve as a brake on our impulsive choices. The desire to avoid acting on impulse will be a reason to develop habits of commitment-keeping, of course. But recognizing the value of such habits will also give one a reason to continue solidifying the habit of acting deliberately moment by moment, and so of adhering to one's commitment.

Relatedly, choosing contrary to the general habit of commitment-keeping when one confronts *accidie* or adversity *ex post* will tend to undermine this habit and make it less available in the future. Presuming it is useful at any point, then, and given its likely fragility, we do well to nurture it rather than to cause it to dissipate.

Keeping a commitment can also serve the general end of cognitive economy. By ruling out certain otherwise possible choices, a commitment keeps me from having to expend time and energy evaluating those choices.[14] Making a commitment with regard to one issue frees me to devote time and energy to considering other issues.

Keeping commitments also matters in a variety of ways in the course of our social interactions, of course. People who know they can count on us will be more inclined to cooperate with us. Of course we want to be thought reliable; but the best way to be *thought* reliable is to *be* reliable. And this means not only that we are reliable promise-keepers but perhaps also that we are reliable as regards our own commitments. If we are known to adhere to our own commitments, others may have reason to judge us to be reliable and so to rely on us.[15]

The habit of commitment also matters in our social interactions because some of our preferences concern the well-being of others, and we can sometimes realize these preferences more effectively if we have developed the habit of being reliable people. But while the habit may matter in our social interactions, it may be difficult to develop the habit of behaving reliably in relation to others while being fickle with respect to those commitments that do *not* invite reliability by others. And, more positively, engaging in reliable behavior with respect to oneself will not only reinforce the habit of reliability generally but also signal one's reliability to others.

Being committed helps to confer greater unity on one's life story. And this will provide added reason for the various segments of that story to matter to one, and for one, to engage in rational action and to plan for the future. To the extent that one wants to be prudent, then, one will have reason to encourage attitudes and habits that make prudence more likely, and so to be committed.[16]

A further reason *ex post* to keep one's commitments is that doing so can be a source of positive regard for oneself.[17] It is notoriously difficult on occasion to act against our immediate impulses and to avoid giving up in the face of adversity. While particular situational goals may come and go, the goal of (justifiably) viewing oneself positively seems likely to persist. Quite apart from the substantive goods to be realized in and through adhering to a particular commitment, there's simply the positive self-assessment that might come with doing something difficult.[18] One will need fortitude to achieve almost any goal. And this means that fortitude will be consistently admirable (ignoring the case in which one is committed to a thoroughly destructive project). Of course this means that one will have reason to seek fortitude in any case, quite apart from its capacity to evoke admiration and respect. And one will increase the likelihood that one will exhibit it precisely by nurturing it over time.

Relatedly, successfully achieving the goals one has set for oneself can be expected to boost one's self-confidence. And self-confidence might be expected to radiate out in a variety of ways, enhancing both others' perceptions of one's capacities and attractiveness and one's ability to complete one's various projects.

People will often, perhaps usually, want to regard themselves positively. But there will be instrumental reasons for people to embrace this preference if they do not already do so. On the view, at any rate, that one really is a self that is unified over time, one may well wish to benefit oneself in the future. But a self one admires will be easier to care about, and so more likely to prompt beneficial action, than a self one does not. So becoming the kind of person who earns one's own admiration by keeping commitments even when doing so is difficult will be a self the satisfaction of whose preferences one is more likely to care about and promote.[19]

Photographer Theron Humphrey provides an interesting example.[20] Humphrey and his rescue dog, Maddie, set out on a yearlong trek across the United States in a Volkswagen mini-van. Humphrey captured images of Maddie interacting with a variety of features of the various environments they encountered in a coffee-table book he's since published.

Humphrey could have undertaken an entirely different project. But he chose to invest a year of his time in a cross-country odyssey and to turn his experience into art. What's interesting is the way he chose to frame his experience with reference to commitment. Focusing on his canine associate, Humphrey says:

> Maddie taught me that I should wake up every morning and be grateful. She taught me that committing to something and sticking to it is how we grow. But most of all, she taught me that standing on things, everyday objects, can be incredible. She's my best friend and I wouldn't trade our time together for anything.[21]

Humphrey evidently committed not only to Maddie but also to the project of working together with her on a book. The commitment mattered not only because it resulted in a particular artistic product but also, if I understand Humphrey correctly, simply because he learned determination and persistence and patience, learned to stick to something he'd planned on doing. Instrumental reason has, in the nature of the case, little or nothing to say about whether Humphrey's *goal* was worthwhile. But it will be instrumentally rational to cultivate the capacity to fulfill one's commitments because of the value of this capacity in so many different circumstances.

Relatedly, one might also see the task of keeping one's commitments as serving to differentiate oneself from others.[22] This might sometimes positively affect one's behavior. And this kind of differentiation, too, may give one a specific reason to care about oneself over time. One might well think that a self with no clear identity, no clear character, was a self not worth caring about, because such a self might make no actual contribution of note to the world—blown about, as it must be, by every passing wind.

Further, given the difficulty of adhering to challenging commitments, doing so will likely result in admiration from others quite unrelated to their reliance on one. One's adherence will likely be seen as manifesting a kind of *strength*, perhaps in some cases physical strength but certainly strength of character, that will elicit their general respect and appreciation. Given the desire to elicit positive attitudes on the part of others, positive attitudes that can be expected to benefit her in a variety of often unforeseen ways, someone reasoning instrumentally will have a further reason to adhere to a challenging commitment if there's some chance it will affect others' perceptions of her.

One may also find it instrumentally useful to keep a commitment because the varying elements of one's life fit together to form a package that hangs together, at least to some degree. A commitment, and the projects undertaken in fulfillment of the commitment, will form part of this package. Reinventing oneself may be costly, and this may be a reason to preserve the package in something like a recognizable form.

There's no way of adhering to the-practice-of-commitment-in-general. Rather, we need to adhere to particular commitments. But doing so can help us to achieve goals quite independent of those the particular commitments seek to serve, both by fostering worthwhile habits and by signaling in relevant ways.

## IV. Rational Commitments

It can make sense to see myself as a self extended over time, with concerns that reach forward and backward from the present moment. If I do see myself in this way, I can certainly have preferences for the states of my future selves, and I can also take into account what I believe the preferences of those future selves will be. Given that I can do so, there will be multiple reasons to make and keep commitments. One will make commitments in order to shape the future in accordance with one's current preferences. One will keep the commitments one has made because those commitments have shaped one's preferences and habits, because they have led to the creation of extrinsic incentives that constrain one's choices, and because doing so will contribute in a variety of ways to helping one achieve not just any goals they happen to embody but also almost any goals one is likely to have.

Seeing commitment-keeping as instrumentally rational presupposes one's ability to understand oneself as a self extended in time. But it needn't involve any judgments about the *value* of one's identity. If, however, one sees achieving or maintaining self-integration as valuable, this will provide further normative reasons for taking commitments seriously. I explore this possibility in Chapter 2.

## Notes

1 On this kind of reasoning, *see, e.g.*, GERALD F. GAUS, ON PHILOSOPHY, POLITICS, AND ECONOMICS 7–29 (2008).
2 *Cf.* PAUL RICOEUR, ONESELF AS ANOTHER 113–68 (Kathleen Blamey trans., 1992); ALASDAIR C. MACINTYRE, AFTER VIRTUE: A STUDY IN MORAL THEORY 215–25 (2d ed. 1984). For a slightly more ambitious proposal, albeit one clearly intended to be fully compatible with philosophical naturalism, *see* JOHN SEARLE, RATIONALITY IN ACTION 79–96 (2001).
3 To be clear, I regard talk of past and future selves as a *façon de parler*.
4 For what follows in Part III, *see generally* ROBERT NOZICK, THE NATURE OF RATIONALITY 9–35 (1993); DAVID SCHMIDTZ, RATIONAL CHOICE AND MORAL AGENCY 2015 at 81, 91–97, 108–119 (2015); JON ELSTER, ULYSSES AND THE SIRENS (1984); JON ELSTER, ULYSSES UNBOUND (2000).
5 *Cf.* ELSTER, SIRENS, *supra* note 4, at 36–111; ELSTER, UNBOUND, *supra* note 4, at 1–87.
6 *See* SCHMIDTZ, *supra* note 4, at 109–12, 117. A further way of affecting the *ex ante* probability that I will behave in a way I desire will be to reframe my situation or my actions; *see* ELSTER, SIRENS, *supra* note 4, at 105–07.
7 Thanks to Blase Harris for calling to my attention the passage from which this quote is drawn.
8 *See* NOZICK, *supra* note 4, at 21–26.
9 *See id.* at 17–19.
10 Describing this strategy as "bunching," Elster suggests that it is fairly clearly effective but questions its rationality. *See* ELSTER, UNBOUND, *supra* note 4, at 84–86. One might, it seems to me, regard the effectiveness of the strategy as counting fairly decisively in favor of the instrumental rationality of employing it.
11 *See* NOZICK, *supra* note 4, at 19–20. Nozick observes that, given weakness of will, I will have reason not to formulate stringent principles from which I will be too likely to defect, since this may undermine my capacity to adhere to principles more generally.
12 *See* SCHMIDTZ, *supra* note 4, at 116–17.
13 *See* NOZICK, *supra* note 4, at 14. *Cf.* MARGARET A. FARLEY, PERSONAL COMMITMENTS 33–37 (1986).
14 *See* NOZICK, *supra* note 4, at 14.
15 Stephen Clark notes (in personal communication) that this is the sort of thing that occurs in G. K. Chesterton's *Tales of the Long Bow*, in which a political party wins an election precisely because its leaders have already demonstrated their reliability in private matters.
16 *See* SCHMIDTZ, *supra* note 4, at 112–13.
17 *See id.* at 114.

18 There will, of course, be varying forms of positive self-assessment; *see, e.g.,* David Sachs, *How to Distinguish Self-Respect from Self-Esteem*, 10 PHIL. PUB. AFF. 346 (1981).
19 *See* SCHMIDTZ, *supra* note 4, at 113–14. Thanks to David Gordon for this reference.
20 *See* Tanja M. Laden, *Maddie on Things*, POP CURIOUS (Apr. 8, 2013), http://popcurious.com/maddie-coonhound (last visited Mar. 7, 2017).
21 *Id.* (quoting Theron Humphrey).
22 *Cf.* NOZICK, *supra* note 4, at 12; SCHMIDTZ, *supra* note 4, at 114.

# 2 Commitment, Identity, and Integrity

*Fulfilling a commitment can be a way of effecting or maintaining self-integration or of embracing an identity not misshaped by failure.*

## I. Commitment and Coherence

Another family of approaches to understanding the significance of commitment focuses on the role of keeping commitments in preserving our integrity and our identities. Integrity here may be a matter of maintaining a coherent *identity* or of maintaining coherence among the choices we make as we plan.

In Part II, I consider the notion that recognizing the value of self-integration offers us good reason to keep our commitments. I suggest that, while it does so, it may do little to show that it is unreasonable to adhere to resolutions that are proving difficult to keep. In Part III, I emphasize that some kinds of commitments, to what Bernard Williams calls "ground projects," may implicate our identities in significant ways and that this may provide some reason to adhere to these commitments in particular. In Part IV, I note that one sort of integrity-based argument for adhering to commitments might focus on the ways in which we create new possibilities for success and failure by making commitments. In Part V, I note the ways in which abandoning our commitments might be inconsistent with the practice of making plans. I conclude with an overview in Part VI.

## II. Commitment and Integrity

Adhering to a commitment may be seen as a way of acknowledging and maintaining one's integrity. Thus, Robert P. George maintains:

> In light of a reasonable personal . . . commitment I have made, it may be perfectly reasonable for me to treat, and, indeed, it may be patently

unreasonable for me to fail to treat, certain basic values or certain possible instantiations of a single basic value as superior to others in their directive force (for me). Choosing in harmony with one's past reasonable commitments, and, thus, establishing or maintaining one's personal integrity . . . constitutes an important moral reason which often guides our choices between rationally grounded options.[1]

The notion of integrity is multifaceted.[2] Sometimes, people talk about integrity as if it were identical with moral resoluteness. Sometimes, integrity is treated as equivalent to being honest and honorable. My concern here, though, is with integrity as *self-integration*, the inner consistency of the elements of one's life-story and of one's choices. Safeguarding integrity is a matter of ensuring both that the elements of one's life over time constitute a coherent whole and that one's feelings, attitudes, and decisions at any given point fit together, too.

Suppose I have made a commitment to behaving in a certain way later. In this case, if I wonder whether to fulfill the commitment, it will be relevant that I *have* made the commitment and that, having made it, I will impede the integration of my personal story if I now ignore it. This will be especially true if, at the time at which I've planned to act, I acknowledge the attraction and the value of the goods I sought to realize by making the commitment in the first place, even if I now also experience the appeal of alternative goods. By choosing to adhere to my commitment, I am preserving my self-integration, solidifying it (given that I am reinforcing the habit of adhering to commitments), and signaling it to myself and others.

We decide who we will be when we make commitments—whether we initiate them deliberately or whether we retrospectively ratify attachments that have emerged unbidden or unplanned. We determine our identities. To disregard these commitments is, then, or can be, to attack our own identities, our own selves.[3] Disregarding a commitment can fracture the life one has created—not just any life, but the life for which one has taken responsibility by *choosing*.

From the perspective of the natural law view I'm inclined to defend, but also from others, including rather less systematic ones, self-integration is an aspect of well-being. And so it will always be intelligible and reasonable (making relevant allowances) to act to achieve or maintain self-integration. Adhering to one's commitments because doing so will foster self-integration, and declining to abandon them because doing *that* would undermine one's self-integration, will always be intelligible and (in the absence of special circumstances) reasonable.[4]

Of course there are aspects of ourselves that *ought* to be rejected. The fact that something is part of my identity does not show definitively that it should claim my loyalty. I can reflect on it in light of the relevant moral requirements to determine whether they rule it out. If they do not, however, I may reasonably embrace my commitment as appropriately identity-constitutive. (Of course, just because I've reasonably accepted something as helping to constitute my identity, it doesn't follow that my identity *should* be protected and preserved. Doing so is valuable, given that self-integration is an aspect of well-being, even if not categorically required.)

While we have reason to value our identities, it isn't the case, except when one has made promises or commitments related to specific goods (or when fairness requires specific benevolent acts), that one acts *un*reasonably when one fails to seek to realize a particular good. So considerations related to self-integration so far show only why recognizing the value of self-integration might make it appealing to adhere to one's commitments. They do not show that declining to do so would be unreasonable.

One may reasonably—on varied theoretical grounds—ignore goods of all sorts, provided one does not treat them as if they were actually valueless. One may, indeed, choose reasonably even when one knows that injury to one or more goods—one's own or another's—will result from one's choices. One may do this, that is, provided that one does not *intend* the injury, that one does not, that is, effect it purposefully or instrumentally, and that acting in a way that—inadvertently but foreseeably—brings it about is consistent with the other requirements of practical reasonableness. It will be *un*reasonable to affect one's self-integration adversely only when one purposefully or instrumentally attacks it or when one does so in a way that is otherwise inconsistent with the requirements of practical reasonableness. Otherwise, one may reasonably act in ways that in fact undermine one's self-integration in one way or another.[5]

Suppose, for instance, that one has over time sedimented an identity as a happy-go-lucky playboy, enjoying a wide range of casual sexual encounters while shunning deeper intimacy. To one's great surprise, one falls in love, and concludes that safeguarding and enriching one's relationship with one's lover requires that one discontinue one's habit of engaging in the casual sex that has heretofore been a staple of one's existence. Choosing to focus exclusively on one's lover will undoubtedly disrupt the continuity of one's life. But one does not choose exclusivity *in order* to disrupt this continuity. One's purpose is not to act against one's own self-integration. Rather, the disruption of one's identity is a foreseen but unintended consequence of choosing exclusivity over variety for the first time.

In this case, of course, I've focused on an identity that one has sedimented just in virtue of making particular choices, choices to structure particular relationships in particular ways. While choosing exclusivity over variety *in this case* is not an attack on self-integration, might it be when one has made choices—commitments—specifically designed to constrain one's future choices, to shape one's future? If one has made a *commitment*, for instance, to being a Don Juan, does one act unreasonably if, after falling in love, one opts instead for exclusivity?

It seems as if having made a commitment won't change an analysis framed in terms of self-integration. Ignoring, altering, abandoning a commitment will, indeed, undermine one's self-integration. But one and the same act may both undermine one's self-integration and support one's relationship with one's lover. One doesn't, in the imagined case, decline to engage in a casual fling one would previously have welcomed *in order* to attack one's self-integration. And one is not choosing to undermine one's self-integration in this way as a means, *per se*, to the solidification of the relationship with one's lover. Rather, the same choices that solidify one's relationship with one's lover also, at the same time, undermine one's self-integration. A person who in fact gives priority to self-integration will for that reason avoid undermining the narrative coherence of her life by disregarding her commitments—self-integration provides her with a reason to do so—but she does not act unreasonably if she does not in a particular case give priority to self-integration in this way.[6]

In the case of the violation of a commitment, the point of the relevant action—say, our imagined Don Juan's decision to embrace exclusivity—is not to shatter the connection between his present and past selves, even if this turns out to happen as a result of the change in his behavior. In some cases, of course, violating a past commitment *will* count as an attack on a basic aspect of well-being. Suppose, for instance, that someone aims at excellence in work and regards breaking with past choices as essential to (her preferred type of) excellence in work. Suppose, too, that some of her relevant past choices qualify as commitments. She might in this case be purposefully attacking her own self-integration. And this certainly *could* qualify as an unreasonable failure to keep a commitment.[7] But this doesn't seem like the most common sort of case. In general, it seems as if acknowledging the value of self-integration could sometimes be consistent with abandoning a commitment.

## III.  Preserving Oneself

Challenging utilitarianism, Bernard Williams observes that

> among the things that make people happy is . . . being taken up or involved in any of a vast range of projects or—if we waive the

evangelical and moralizing associations of the word—commitments. One can be committed to such things as a person, a cause, an institution, a career, one's own genius, or the pursuit of danger.[8]

There is considerable, if perhaps not perfect, overlap between Williams's talk here of commitments, as, in effect, synonymous with *projects*, and his discussion elsewhere of *ground projects*.[9] Not all projects will be ground projects, and it seems unlikely that all commitments in Williams's will be, either. However, Williams's discussion of ground projects suggests a particular sort of reason why we might adhere to those commitments that are, in fact, ground projects.

For Williams, the point is not so much the maintenance of a coherent identity, not so much a matter of internal consistency (even if many of his concerns might be cashed this way), but rather a matter of taking seriously what gives a point to one's life. He introduces the idea of ground projects in connection with (one version of) his critique of moral impartiality. A ground project can, he suggests, give purpose and meaning to someone's life. Engaging in this project will then be a precondition of her acting at all. And so it will be unreasonable to suppose that she should give it up in the name of impartial morality, given that without it her life will lose its meaning.

If Williams's arguments are persuasive, not much will follow with regard to many of the choices or configurations of the self that I have in mind when talking about commitments. In the narrow sense with which I was concerned in Part II, ignoring a commitment might fracture one's identity. However, on the natural law view that's been in the background of what I've argued to date, it might be perfectly acceptable to act in a way that, as a matter of fact, resulted in the fracturing of one's identity.

Williams seems to have something more dramatic in mind. To abandon a ground project is not merely to chip away at one's identity at the edges but to let go of who one is in a decisive way. As Williams notes, this need not mean that the end of a ground project makes suicide one's only option,[10] but one might perfectly well find one's life sapped of meaning; one might well think that one really had, in effect, died.

One will be disposed not to abandon a ground project, then, because doing so will sap one's life of meaning. And perhaps it will not even make sense to ask whether, if one is tempted to abandon the project, one *should* resist the temptation. For built into the structure of one's action and feeling and judgment will be the resources to resist it. One could only treat this sort of temptation as worth acceding to if the ground project *failed* to provide one's life with meaning. It is not, perhaps, strictly impossible for someone to say, "This gives my life meaning, but I think I'll abandon it for the sake of some transitory satisfaction," but it seems, at minimum, profoundly difficult psychologically to reach a point at which this was a viable option. For, if someone *did* say this, our first instinct would be to suspect that the project being abandoned did not, in fact, confer much in the way of meaning on her life. The idea of a project's giving meaning to one's life is precisely that it provides motivation and justification for one's continued action, potentially in the face of great adversity, across a range of contexts and through a range of periods. A project that could be readily abandoned would not be one that offered the relevant kind of meaning.

Different projects might offer one different sorts of meaning. And so one might intelligibly replace one ground project with another, perhaps having concluded that something was deeply amiss about the project being replaced—perhaps it rested on a serious factual error or, alternatively, perhaps fulfilling it involved engaging in thoroughly unethical conduct. And simply to acknowledge these deficiencies might be utterly devastating. If, however, in tandem with recognizing them one simultaneously embraced some other project—perhaps one that drew on many of the same energies and relationships—one might, indeed, abandon the initial project without finally devastating loss.

In any case, when a commitment is or issues in a ground project in Williams's sense, the inescapability of the quest for meaning will provide one with one sort of reason to retain the commitment. One might think that, while meaning could be found in a wide range of places, *some* source of meaning was essential to going on from day to day in life. And one might further judge that, having embraced a source of meaning, *abandoning* or *rejecting* that source of meaning would be profoundly devastating to one's sense of self and one's sense of purpose, so that there was a kind of bootstrapping reason to retain any ground project once embraced.

Of course, this will not be the only reason for retaining one's commitment to a ground project. For there will also be the sense that the project has entered deeply and constitutively into one's motivations and one's sense of who one is. It will not simply be the case, then, that rejecting it will mean a loss of ongoing *purpose* in life but also that it will result in a deformation, a disfigurement, a distortion or diminution of the self no less serious, and perhaps much more serious, than the loss of a body part.

We are, of course, vulnerable to profound loss when we embrace such projects. It does not follow, however, that we should avoid them in order to immunize ourselves against the risk of loss. For something can offer me a great gift only, it seems, if being deprived of it can amount to a great loss. To give up or avoid the possibility of being hurt by losing a ground project (a relationship, an activity, or whatever else might constitute the project) is to give up at the same time the possibility of being profoundly *enriched* by the project. The project can make my life much better only, in short, if losing it has the potential to make my life much worse. There are things worse than suffering and loss, and it makes little sense to treat avoiding them as the most important constraint on one's choices.

This does not mean, of course, that there is no value in the *detachment* that various moral and spiritual traditions—from Stoicism to Christian monasticism to Buddhism—have recommended. But detachment in the useful sense doesn't mean embracing the absurd judgment that nothing matters (if it doesn't, then the goods purportedly achievable through detachment wouldn't matter, either, and so would provide no reason for avoiding passionate, vulnerable engagement). Nor does it mean adopting the slightly less absurd judgment that nothing matters very much. Nor again, perhaps more controversially, does it mean accepting the thought that one's identity, the value and meaning of one's life, or one's emotional stance vis-à-vis the world should be unaffected by what happens with regard to one's projects, given that embracing this thought would mean denying oneself the chance to experience the joy and elation that importantly signal the value of one's experiences and achievements.

Instead, the point of detachment in the useful sense is that my projects, important as they are to me, while they provide me with perfectly good reasons for action, do not for this reason justify me in giving in to the temptation to seek to control others in order to fulfill them, to ignore the independent value and reality of those who almost unavoidably will need to play parts in those projects. While my projects are important to me, they are not so overwhelmingly important that their value trumps the value of everything else in my deliberation. Being appropriately detached from them doesn't mean *abandoning* them but, rather, not *absolutizing* them. The point of detachment is to recognize that no one's value or reality is or could or should be exhausted by whatever role she or he might be able to play in my projects and, indeed, that I am not entitled to expect that others will cooperate with me on my own terms and submit to my demands whatever their own projects. It is also to acknowledge that, even where free creatures aren't concerned, I am ultimately incapable of controlling the rest of the world, and it makes no sense to respond emotionally to developments in the world as if I could. Detachment in the relevant sense means accepting and respecting the independent agency of others, the fact that they have their own projects that are often entirely independent of, and sometimes at odds with, my own, and the independent reality, more generally, of everything other than myself.[11]

The temptation to seek to control other creatures or aspects of reality will be greater in proportion to the extent to which the projects in which I have assigned them roles are crucial to my own sense of meaning and selfhood. But of course no one else can be expected to submerge her- or himself in my projects at the loss of her or his own identity. And no one, no matter how committed, can guarantee that she or he will be able to sustain my projects through her or his own involvement. People die. They go mad. They lose their capacity to play football. And so forth. The injunction to practice detachment is best understood, then, as the injunction to acknowledge this inescapable feature of reality and to avoid raging impotently at it if it intervenes between oneself and the realization of one's projects.

There's no reason to avoid committing to ground projects. But we must recognize that doing so will unavoidably involve the potentially terrifying vertigo that accompanies the risk of loss. And we must acknowledge that a ground project cannot exhaust one's responsibilities even if it evacuates many of them of meaning.

I will have deeply rooted reasons to embrace and persist in those commitments that subserve or constitute my ground projects, if I have any. As long as the commitments involve such projects, ennui will be unlikely to overtake me where they are concerned, given their constitutive role in relation to my identity and their crucial maintenance of my sense of meaning. Here, the challenge will not be to persist in my commitments—that I must do so in such a case may seem so inescapably obvious that any alternative may be inconceivable—but rather to do so without resisting the reality of others' projects and other facets of the world or of the other values my actions may realize or otherwise affect.

## IV. Avoiding Failure

We have good reason to want to avoid failure. Abandoning or not fulfilling our commitments is a clear instance of failure. So we have good reason to want to avoid abandoning or not fulfilling our commitments.[12]

A *habit* of loyalty or self-investment, or, alternatively, a *principle* of loyalty or self-investment, can't be abandoned without consequences. In the first case, these will be, at minimum, psychological: to act contrary to a habit is to make it harder to exhibit the original habit in the future, particularly since one has, by one's choice, begun to form the habit of declining to be loyal or to self-invest in particular circumstances. Similarly, one cannot consistently treat a putative requirement of loyalty or self-investment *as a requirement* in a given case if one has come to reject its authority in a relevantly similar case (unless one now declines to endorse the earlier decision). One can act as the requirement would in fact dictate, of course, but in so doing one isn't treating it as authoritative. And of course abandoning the habit or the principle will have consequences for one's ability to engage in various sorts of practices in the future.[13]

To experience oneself as an agent is to take one's life to be in some meaningful sense under one's own direction. Identifying with one's life, experiencing it as one's own, might seem to involve this sort of self-ascription of agency. And this means, in turn, that one's identity as an agent can be called into question when one doesn't continue with one's plans. One makes a decision to proceed in a certain way, but one then gives up. So one's initial decision seems inefficacious, even pointless. Having set a goal for oneself, and perhaps a path leading to that goal, one has now *failed*. "The more failures one accumulates in one's important pursuits the more of a failure one's life becomes."[14]

Obviously, most of our commitments are not unqualified and unconditional. They include various qualifiers and escape clauses.[15] Even allowing for this, however, in making a commitment one sets a goal for oneself, and thus establishes a new possibility, the possibility of success or failure. Presuming one has, in the first place, made a genuine commitment, then failing to adhere to it is inconsistent with one's initial choice: one has set oneself a task only to fail.[16] As an autonomous agent, one determines the contours of one's life by means of one's commitments. From among things that have the potential to enrich one's life and the lives of others, one selects particular goods on which one will focus, goods one will embrace, so that they become not just valuable in general but *one's own values*.[17] Thus, one's life can go wrong, one can fail, when one doesn't adhere to those commitments.[18]

Someone will certainly have reason to regret failure. (*i*) If she fails, she will have set a goal for herself only to go on to demonstrate that she lacks the skill or determination needed to achieve it (or both), and this will reflect badly on her self-understanding and others' understandings of her. (*ii*) But the problem is not just that she lacks these qualities—whose absence from her life might be evident in a variety of contexts other than the pursuit of the goals she's set for herself. It's also that she hasn't *reached* an objective she's set for herself. But of course *this* could happen without any lapse in capacity or character: she might prepare for a competition with all the determination imaginable, only to be bested by an even better competitor; or she might be about to achieve an important objective just at the moment some exogenous event interrupts her progress. Failure will be something she has reason to regret, then, even apart from the ways in which it might reflect on her capacities. (*iii*) It seems as if her failure will be rendered particularly troubling and regrettable because of the *confluence* of these factors. She has not achieved her goal *and* she hasn't done so because she didn't perform in the needed way. She is not only missing out on the good she sought to realize but she can now also see herself as the kind of person who gives up too soon or invests insufficiently to achieve her own objectives.

The failure to be true to oneself is not just an instance—though it *is* an instance—of failure at self-integration. I may not succeed at integrating a set of conflicting impulses into a coherent plan for what I'll do personally or professionally during a given month, for instance. But the fact that I haven't isn't any sort of failure to be loyal or faithful. The thought that I've failed to be true to myself implies that I've ignored an aspect of my identity that has normative weight. Something might begin simply as an attachment of one kind or another—something that simply develops, perhaps even something that feels as if it's just *happened* to me. But when I come to accept it, to ratify it, it becomes not merely a part of my psychic makeup or my social environment but also an aspect of my identity. By *choosing* it in this way, committing to it in this way, I elect to make it part of who I am. And this is the sense in which rejecting it means rejecting part of myself, so that affirming and maintaining it is, in turn, a way of being true to myself. Choosing it in this way thus creates the possibility of normatively significant failure.

## V. Fulfilling Our Plans

Treating commitments as revisable at will is hard to square with the point of planning or committing.[19]

### A. A Principle of Commitment

Suppose I think of myself as considering several possible versions of a principle that will guide my choices related to the commitments I've made.[20]

1.  Don't make commitments.
2.  Make commitments, but feel free to ignore them at will.
3.  Make commitments, but keep them sporadically.
4.  Make commitments and keep them.[21]

I would deprive myself of the ability to realize valuable goods if I declined to make commitments entirely. I would be limited to participating in those goods that presented themselves to me moment by moment and in those I happened to be disposed to pursue on a more extended basis. Accepting (1) would deprive me of a range of worthwhile options, and it is hard to see that it would be rational for me to accept it.

But accepting (2) would seem likely to result in my incurring similar liabilities. We don't want, obviously, to eliminate spontaneity from our lives, and across large swaths of action and experience we might well want the freedom to change our minds at will. But to adopt (2) is to take up this stance with regard to *all* of the arenas of our lives. We can obviously build in the freedom to act on impulse when we make particular—obviously quite weak—commitments. But (2) places much stronger limits on our commitments: to accept (2) is to accept that *every* commitment will be limited by impulse, even when we consciously, deliberately choose that it not be. It is hard to see how an intention I thought about in this way could even *qualify* as a commitment. Rather, it seems as if adopting (2) would just mean abandoning the possibility of making commitments entirely.[22]

If one accepted (3), one could make *some* commitments, but one would, it seems, treat others rather as adopting (2) would mean one treated all commitments. Accepting (3) would certainly make planning possible and it would enable one to reap some of the benefits of committing. But it seems as if one would deprive oneself of those benefits in the cases in which one treats commitments as capable of being abandoned at will. And, again, it would seem as if those were really cases in which one wasn't making commitments at all.

What might place some putative commitments in the category of those that might be sporadically abandoned? If this is purely random, one's capacity to plan and to reap the benefits of commitment will be seriously undermined. If it's a matter of impulse, then it seems as if (3) will encounter the same sorts of difficulties as (2), since any case in which I feel an impulse to alter or abandon a commitment will be one in which I do so. If it's a matter of desired spontaneity, this can presumably be built into a particular commitment or class of commitments from the beginning, in which case (to anticipate) (3) becomes indistinguishable from (4).

It seems as if accepting (4) will enable one to experience the evident benefits of commitment. It will not be undermined by the inner contradiction that seems to dog the hells of (2) and (3). And it can certainly allow for the kind of flexibility that will prevent commitments from being unnecessarily rigid and inhospitable to spontaneity, since necessarily presupposed, contingently assumed, or explicitly noted constraints can be built into one's commitments.

These will, of course, include constraints related to considerations of which one was ignorant or to which one gave insufficient attention when one made the commitment. They will not, by contrast, include factors one actually did consider when one made the commitment and which one rejected as defeaters for the commitment. For the exclusion of these factors was, *ex hypothesi*, built into the commitment itself, and to treat them as decisive now would be, in effect, to reject one's commitment (which includes the commitment not to act in light of these factors) on impulse, and so to act in accordance with (2).

If (4) is the most rational principle to follow with respect to commitments, I have reason to affirm it at each moment when I am considering or making a decision. It therefore seems as if I act irrationally when I disregard my commitments at will.

## B. *Responsibility over Time*

Another way to get at the point might look like this. We need to be able to plan for the future. But we cannot do so if we cannot count on ourselves to carry out the plans we adopt. There will be no point in making plans, and so in even beginning to fulfill them, if we cannot rely on our future selves to continue them. Each of us wants to be able to make plans, and so to rely on her or his future self to carry them out. And each of us *is* a future self to multiple past selves *and* a past self to multiple future selves. Any particular plan I've made in the present may come into effect in the future; and at this point I will not need to rely on my future self with respect to *this* plan. But I will, of course, need to do so with respect to other, still-future, plans. It will be inconsistent of me to expect my future selves to be reliable, to believe it would be wrong or inappropriate or unreasonable or undesirable for them to be unreliable, while declining to prove reliable for my own past selves.[23]

When we plan, when we commit, we project our decisions, our wills, our selves into the future. We seek to determine who we will be. And being able to do this is thoroughly useful at multiple points. We do not act irrationally just because we opt for one good rather than another. But the value of being able to shape our futures deliberately and the links between our past, present, and future selves give us reason to avoid opting for one good on impulse when we have already committed to another.

## VI. Integrating Ourselves Through Commitment

Concerns with integrity and identity provide multiple reasons to make and keep commitments. Making commitments enables us to define our identities, to embrace projects that help to confer meaning on our lives, to make particular goods our own, and to achieve medium- and long-term goals. Keeping commitments, in turn, is a way of affirming the value of integrated life-stories and, on occasion, of avoiding unreasonable attacks on our identities. This is a powerful reason insofar as self-integration matters. But it is not, on its face, unreasonable to disregard self-integration in order to flourish in some way that might tend to undermine it. However, we have other reasons for keeping commitments. Doing so helps to preserve meaning in our lives (though of course many of our commitments aren't sources of profound meaning). It enables us to avoid marring our life stories with failure. And it embodies a crucial willingness to choose and act consistently: the consistency not only of our identities but also of our activities as planners matters as well in making it unreasonable to abandon our commitments.

Self-integration is potentially one aspect of the well-being of creatures like ourselves. But there is reason to think that there are many such aspects, all of them incommensurable. If there are, indeed, diverse, incommensurable dimensions of flourishing, this might suggest additional reasons for making and keeping commitments. I consider what these might be in Chapter 3.

## Notes

1  *Cf.* ROBERT P. GEORGE, IN DEFENSE OF NATURAL LAW 94 (1999).
2  For an extended and illuminating discussion, *see* David Bauman, Integrity, Identity, and Why Moral Exemplars Do What Is Right (2011) (unpublished Ph.D. dissertation, Washington University—St. Louis).
3  *See* JOSEPH RAZ, VALUE, RESPECT, AND ATTACHMENT 34 (2001).
4  In this and the immediately following paragraphs, I am spelling out the implications of the NCNL view as I would be inclined to understand and defend it. But I think the idea that we cannot avoid adversely affecting all aspects of well-being all the time is one that will make sense from a variety of normative perspectives.
5  On the general question of foreseeably but unintentionally causing adverse effects, *see, e.g.*, Germain Grisez, *Toward a Consistent Natural-Law Ethics of Killing*, 15 AM. J. JURIS. 64 (1970); Joseph M. Boyle, *Toward Understanding the Principle of Double Effect*, 90 ETHICS 527 (1980); WARREN QUINN, MORALITY AND ACTION 175–97 (1993). Thanks to David Gordon for comments on this point.
6  To note the obvious, this will still be true, *if self-integration provides the only reason to keep commitments*, even should she have *committed* herself to giving priority to self-integration.
7  Thanks to David Gordon for this example.
8  BERNARD WILLIAMS, *A Critique of Utilitarianism*, in UTILITARIANISM: FOR AND AGAINST 75, 112 (J. J. C. Smart & Bernard Williams eds., 1973).
9  *See* BERNARD WILLIAMS, *Persons, Character and Morality*, in THE IDENTITIES OF PERSONS 197, 209–15 (Amélie Oksenberg Rorty ed., 1976).
10  *See* WILLIAMS, *Persons, supra* note 9, at 209.
11  I owe this view of detachment to Nicholas Lash. On concerns about ground projects, *cf.* ROBERT MERRIHEW ADAMS, FINITE AND INFINITE GOODS: A FRAMEWORK FOR ETHICS 207–08 (1999).
12  *See generally* JOSEPH RAZ, THE MORALITY OF FREEDOM 353–55, 385–89 (1986).
13  *See id.* at 355. I speak of *commitments* throughout here, in view of my practice throughout this book, though Raz seems to have in mind a more specific use of the term when he employs it.
14  *See id.* at 383. Thanks to Tanja M. Laden for discussion on this point.
15  *See id.* at 384.
16  *See id.* at 385–86.
17  *Cf.* RAZ, VALUE, *supra* note 3, at 19–20.
18  *See* RAZ, MORALITY, *supra* note 12, at 387.
19  *See* MARK C. MURPHY, NATURAL LAW AND PRACTICAL RATIONALITY 209–11, 268 n.21 (1999).

20  Note that I'm not asking whether I should or shouldn't freely commit to one of these principles, but, rather, which one it will be the most rational to accept.

21  "Keeping a commitment" here will include attending to the limitations built into that particular commitment and those that are presupposed by all commitments.

22  My concern here is with normative rather than causal questions. But it is worth reemphasizing a point I made in Chapter 1. To make what one understood to be genuine commitments while judging that one can abandon it at will, without good reason, would mean that one was not making *commitments* at all—and might not, indeed, be *able* to do so. One would have undercut the availability of the very category of *commitment* by coming to treat commitments as capable of being abandoned or altered at will. If one ignores constraints one has built into a commitment itself from the beginning (*e.g.*, the constraint that I will not discontinue the run I've begun to train for a half-marathon just because I'm quite tired by the sixth mile), one is undercutting one's capacity to commit at all.

23  Stephen Clark notes (in personal communication) the parallel with Aristotle's account of the wicked as always at odds with themselves, lacking secure policies or end-directed identities.

# 3   Commitment and Basic Goods

*Commitments enable us to shape our identities by experiencing the richness and depth of particular instances of the varied, incommensurable aspects of well-being and to establish priorities among them in ways that equip us rationally to plan.*

## I. Starting with Basic Aspects and Instances of Fulfillment

When we make commitments, we choose among different goods—different aspects of flourishing, fulfillment, welfare, or well-being. As I noted in the Introduction, we might think of the basic aspects of well-being, the basic goods, as including life and bodily well-being, knowledge, practical reasonableness, play, friendship and sociability, æsthetic experience, imaginative immersion, meaning and harmony with reality in the widest sense, sensory pleasure, and self-integration and inner peace.[1] These goods are *incommensurable* in a fairly strong sense—incapable of being measured on a common scale and compared quantitatively with each other—and individual instances of each good appear to be non-fungible—incapable of being substituted for each other without loss. We need commitments, in the sense in which I am concerned with them here, in order to embrace these goods and make rational plans with respect to them.

A full-orbed account of flourishing can be seen as building on the recognition that our fulfillment is *constituted* by its diverse aspects. That is, flourishing isn't something other than all the particular ways in which we flourish. This sort of account can be seen as *welfarist* because it focuses on the well-being of actual agents.[2] But it doesn't seek to reduce well-being to desire or appreciation. Desire may be a pointer that allows us to *identify* aspects of well-being, but it does not *constitute* them. Thus, there will be, on the view I'm defending here, a correct and interesting answer to the question whether any given desire is *worth* pursuing.

In what follows, I offer some considerations that might be thought to support the view that the basic goods are inherently valuable and that they're incommensurable and non-fungible, as well as thinking about the links between this view and a plausible understanding of making and keeping commitments. In Part II, I seek to explain why we might regard the basic aspects of well-being as incommensurable. In Part III, I show how the idea of commitment can be seen as a reasonable response to the incommensurability of the basic goods. In Part IV, I seek to show how commitment might figure in a defense of belief in the incommensurability of basic goods against a common objection; I go on to consider some other objections to incommensurability in Part V. I sum up in Part VI.

## II. Incommensurable Basic Goods

Ethics is concerned with well-being—welfare, flourishing, fulfillment. Well-being, in turn, seems to involve activities, relationships, experiences, and achievements that are valuable to us for what they *are*, and not, or not merely, because of our reactions to them. And inherently valuable aspects of welfare seem to be incommensurable, while individual instances of these goods present themselves as non-fungible.

### A. Morality and Living Well

Moral requirements are, I believe, by definition, overriding: a moral requirement is a decisive reason for choice. But that isn't as interesting a claim as it might seem to be. Sometimes, when it's posed, the question is understood to be about whether altruistic, other-regarding considerations always trump self-regarding considerations, or whether impartial considerations trump ones that concern particular loyalties, attachments, commitments, or projects. And the answer to each of *these* questions is surely "no." When I say that morality is overriding, I simply mean that there is, or can be, a (more or less) correct judgment about whether it's bad or unreasonable or unwise, all things considered, to choose in a certain way in a particular situation.

If someone reaches an all-things-considered judgment about her choices with regard to her own flourishing and others', a judgment she takes to be warranted in some (at least moderately) objective way, then she is, in my sense, making a moral judgment. Morality is not simply or primarily a device for securing cooperation. It is concerned with our own well-being, as well as our relationships with those incapable of cooperating or unwilling to cooperate. Thus, if it turns out to be appropriate to choose in a way that realizes the good of æsthetic experience rather than friendship in a particular case, the judgment that it is appropriate will be a moral judgment, even if no one else's well-being is involved.

There is no single, tidy function of morality more interestingly specific than "living well." One way to get at what "living well" might mean is to proceed *in via*, with the recognition that we pursue a broad range of goals.[3] These goals may be seen as *candidates* for endorsement; they may or may not survive reflective scrutiny.[4] That's because I don't value something under the description "object valued by me." I value it because I regard it as worthwhile—as contributing to my welfare or another's. My valuing it *presupposes* my apprehension of it as valuable. What we want are actual achievements, real relationships, not just the semblance of achievements or relationships or the positive mental states evoked by those achievements or relationships.[5] We prize our goals because of their actual worth (as we apprehend it). We don't do it simply, if at all, because they involve particular reactions or experiences.[6]

## B. Being Valuable and Being Valued

It's a common, everyday experience for us to value something for its own sake—not because we believe it will produce something else worthwhile but because whatever it is seems valuable on its own. Think about your desire to contemplate a beautiful painting in a museum, for instance. There may be any number of reasons why you might want to go to a museum: to go on a date, to get out of the house, to enjoy the museum's café. But choosing to contemplate the painting seems to make sense entirely on its own; while you might examine it in order to achieve some other goal (to pass an examination in an art history class, say), you wouldn't *need* to appeal to anything else to explain your attention to it, either to yourself or to anyone else.

Obviously, someone might be able to tell an interesting story about the ways in which creatures like us came to enjoy looking at paintings. But this causal story, a story about the role looking at paintings played in the lives of our distant ancestors, doesn't *explain away* your valuation of the painting for its own sake. At most, it explains how we came to do just what it seems we're actually doing: valuing the painting for its own sake.

For some state of affairs $S$ to be valu*able* is for $S$ to be such that there are considerations that count in favor of valuing $S$. So one can always ask of anything valued for its own sake whether it is, in fact, *valuable*, whether it's *worth valuing*, whether there are, in fact, considerations in virtue of which one ought to value it. To be sure, it could turn out that everything we valued was worth valuing, perhaps just because we valued it. But the notion of being valuable, a normative notion, seems at first blush to be quite different from the notion of being valued, a descriptive one. The set of valued things and the set of valuable things would thus seem, *prima facie*, to be different. And we know that there are all sorts of ways in which things come to be valued; it would be odd indeed if all of them just happened to yield preferences for things actually worth valuing.

The only circumstance in which this wouldn't be the case would be one in which anything valued was necessarily valuable, and it is hard to see what could account for this apart from its being the case that anything valuable was valuable just in virtue of being valued. But presumably one values something in virtue of its particular features. One can't value something in virtue of its being valued, since the choice or disposition to value, to prize, needs to have some justification—to say otherwise would be to be caught in an infinite regress. But since I don't value things in virtue of their being valued, the notion that this is what makes them *valuable*, the notion that the valuable just *is* the valued, can only make sense on the view that what makes something worth valuing is *always* different, and necessarily so, from that in virtue of which anyone actually values it.

This seems logically possible. But it also seems puzzling. Why *should* anyone value anything, on this view? When I value something, I take myself to want it for some feature that is itself worthwhile to me. But the experience of valuing something, the disposition to value it, is a feature, not of the valued object, but of *myself*. Thus, it will always make sense to ask whether this disposition is one I should endorse, one on which I should act, whether I have independently specifiable reasons for doing so. We ordinarily take ourselves to have such *reasons* for valuing things, after all. And if there are such reasons, then the reasons germane in particular cases to my valuing something will be all I need to advert to when talking about why it's valuable: they will *justify* my valuing it. If this is the case, it will be odd to think of my valuing as adding anything else to the story, or as not requiring justification in terms of the reasons that make what I value worth valuing.[7]

Either there are some things worth valuing for themselves or else the notion of something's being valuable, including being valuable *because valued*, simply doesn't make sense. If we grant that it makes sense to regard something as worth valuing *because* it is valued, then we seem able to make sense of the idea of something's being worth valuing. And, if this is the cases, then we might well be able to see things *other* than the actually valued as worth valuing. As a result, much of the appeal of the attempt to understand value in terms of valuation begins to dissipate, since, at minimum, it won't provide a generally applicable account of what's valuable.[8]

## C. Welfare and Happiness

On an alternative view, any action we perform is undertaken for the sake of happiness. On this view, there's *always* an ulterior reason for looking at the painting, helping a friend, playing a game, learning a new skill: we want to be happy. But this claim seems either obviously false or else true in a fairly trivial sense.

If we understand happiness as a particular psychic state, a state in which one is elated, up, or even just aware of being satisfied, it seems apparent that we don't always act in pursuit of such a state, that we often do things that don't, and that we don't expect to, produce happiness. When we act, we're simply not thinking, most of the time, *I'm going to do this in order to* feel *happy*. In addition, feeling happy seems to presuppose something worth feeling *happy about*, something to feel *satisfied by*. Happiness doesn't seem to be the final justification for anything, but, rather, a pointer to something we take to be inherently valuable. Nor will it, therefore, ordinarily be the ultimate explanation for any reasonable action. Of course, I might view a particular painting knowing that it will lift my spirits; I'm not claiming that no one ever does this, or could do this. But this isn't always the case, and it doesn't *need* to be the case to make contemplating the painting intelligible.

This isn't to deny, of course, that we may well come initially, instinctively, to appreciate particular things as sources of subjective pleasure. Surely we do—and it's vital that we do so when we lack the ability or opportunity to deliberate about our choices: sensory signals serve as invaluable cognitive shortcuts that tell us whether some things will conduce to our well-being.[9] But, over time, we learn to detach our preferences for and assessments of the various activities, accomplishments, experiences, and relationships we consider realizing from their roles in the production of the various sensory signals that initially drew us to them or validate our choosing them. We can acknowledge the role of subjective satisfaction in shaping our habits, perceptions, and responses without identifying happiness as what makes particular goods valuable.

On the other hand, suppose we take happiness to be simply welfare, well-being, fulfillment, flourishing. It was once common to use "happiness" to translate the Greek *eudaimonia*, which seems to have had roughly this meaning. In this case, we can see contemplating the painting, say, as a *constituent* of happiness. It's not a *means* to happiness, but a *way of being happy*—that is, a way of flourishing or of being fulfilled, a way in which one's life can go well.

Happiness in this sense doesn't have to involve any particular psychic state.[10] Of course, it *might*: I might well be satisfied, or elated, or delighted, or excited by my contemplation of a painting, my participation in a game, or my interaction with a friend. But here the positive psychological state is an *accompaniment* to my activity or achievement, signaling my awareness that I'm accomplishing what I've sought to accomplish. What I'm satisfied by is the accomplishment itself, which suggests, precisely, that I value the accomplishment for its own sake. Indeed, my satisfaction *is* an instance of my valuing the accomplishment for its own sake.

I cannot prove, of course, that my conscious choice to view the painting for the sake, simply, of the æsthetic experience of viewing the painting really explains my action. Perhaps in reality I'm viewing the painting because of some currently unconscious motive or, indeed, some brain process occurring entirely outside the sphere of conscious awareness. But while this is certainly possible, and while there is certainly evidence of multiple conscious and unconscious constraints on our deliberation and action, still, absent particular evidence that this is the case, it seems to me that I'm entitled to trust my experience. And, of course, unconscious forces that simply *explained* my reaction to the painting causally wouldn't change the nature or quality of my valuation. Offering a plausible causal story *explaining* my valuation of the painting for its own sake doesn't amount to showing, somehow, that I *don't* value the painting for its own sake. And if unconscious motives of one kind or another *supplemented* my valuation of the painting for its own sake, this might mean that my valuation wasn't the only thing responsible for my contemplation of the painting, but it wouldn't show that my valuation *wasn't* my valuation, that I didn't, in fact, regard the painting as valuable for its own sake, rather than for its capacity to produce some psychic state or other.

## D.  *The Appearance of Incommensurability and Non-Fungibility*

Whether or not some features of existence are worth valuing as dimensions of well-being, it's clear that we *experience* ourselves as pursuing a broad range of diverse goals—objects, experiences, activities, relationships—for their own sakes.[11] We don't experience or understand them as valuable because they promote or can be reduced to other things. They present themselves to us as diverse, heterogeneous, just as their individual instances present themselves to us as non-fungible.

Think about something you value—a particular friendship, say. Does it seem to you that you value the friendship *for* something else? Does the friendship matter to you because it's a source of pleasure or money or anything else, or does it matter for its own sake? Suppose it *does* matter for its own sake, that its value isn't reducible to anything else. Its value doesn't seem to be reducible to anything else and doesn't seem to be the same as the value of anything else. Friendship doesn't matter because it is an instance of æsthetic experience or because it produces knowledge, and it's not reducible to life and bodily well-being or to play. Nor is it an instance of or a means to some generic good like pleasure or welfare,[12] since talk about welfare (or fulfillment or flourishing) is just a simple way of talking about all the ways in which things can go well. It seems, therefore, as if friendship and other goods are incommensurable. They can't be compared quantitatively. There's no scale on which friendship and knowledge, say, can both be measured, because these goods don't reduce to or subserve anything that can be used as a basis for quantitative comparison. As Owen Flanagan reminds us, "the goods at which we aim are plural and resist a unifying analysis."[13]

Similarly, *individual* friendships don't seem to matter just as instances of a broader category. Rather, each appears to be valuable in itself, for its own sake. It's unique and irreplaceable. And this gives us good reason to think of it as non-fungible, as incapable of being replaced without loss by some other friendship (or some other good). People's "goods are not necessarily substitutable," Bernard Williams notes. And "[t]hat there must be something which constitutes compensation for a finite loss is just a dogma, one which is more familiar in the traditional version to the effect that every man has his price."[14]

### E. Incommensurability and Maximization

It's worth noting one key implication of the view that the basic goods are incommensurable. Many commonly advocated patterns of reasoning, including those defended by some consequentialists and some proponents of rational-choice models of decision making, assume that it ought to be possible to generate objective quantitative rankings of the states of affairs that are potential objects of choice. But the attempt to maximize makes sense only if there's a quantity to maximize. And it does not in fact seem that there is any such quantity underlying the goods we're in a position to choose: there are only multiple reasons to do various things, not some maximizable master value that underlies those reasons.

If the goods realized in different situations are heterogeneous and if they don't reduce to or subserve some single good, then it does not seem as if it could be possible to produce objective rankings. Absent a common substrate or a shared substantive, quantifiable goal, it is not clear what could make objective quantitative comparisons between goods or clusters of goods possible on a systematic basis. Maximizing and similar strategies seem likely, therefore, to be non-viable.

Thus, Williams highlights "the notorious problem of comparing and adding utilities."[15] Treating happiness in the relevant sense as a matter of "people's desires or preferences and their getting what they want or prefer,"[16] Williams acknowledges skepticism about the idea that "utilities and preference schedules can possibly be all that we are concerned with, even under the heading of individual welfare." This suggests that, *even at the individual level*, the various elements of people's welfare "may not be homogeneous."[17]

Williams supposes that, while this might really be a problem in the case of social choice, "[i]t would be idle to pretend that in many more restricted connexions we had *no idea* what course would lead to greater happiness."[18] But once our focus is on the various heterogeneous aspects of people's well-being, it is less clear that the notion of greater or lesser well-being, *simpliciter*, is even coherent. There is no objective quantity that amounts to the aggregate value of this æsthetic experience, this friendship, this item of knowledge, and all the other instances of welfare embodied in a particular state of affairs. And if there is no objective quantity, there cannot, in general, be any quantitative comparison of the welfare realized in different states of affairs, whether for individual choosers, for groups, or for institutions, so there cannot be any quantity available for maximization.

## III. Commitment and Incommensurability

Recognizing that there are multiple, incommensurable goods gives us several reasons to make and keep commitments. Commitments help to define the self through participation in particular goods while enabling us to participate in basic goods deeply and richly. And commitments make it possible for us to plan.[19]

### A. *Commitment, Self-Definition, and Discovery*

We confront an immense variety of possibilities. We could, in principle, attempt to sample all of them briefly. We would be, in effect, protean selves, constantly shifting, refocusing, moving along the pathway of life in serpentine fashion—veering, turning, redefining. If we are to seek the good of self-integration, however, if we want our lives to hang together, then we have every reason to attend to some goods, realize some possibilities, rather than others. And to do this, we need to commit. It is not enough, obviously, to *choose* among particular goods; we do that unavoidably. But if we are to have stable and coherent identities, and if we are to experience the real richness of particular goods, we need to *invest* on a more extended basis.

This means that we need to make commitments—and at least sometimes extensive ones—with respect to our participation in various aspects of well-being because, if we don't do so, we won't be in a position to flourish in another way. It's not just that commitments allow us to define our identities and render ourselves coherent, and so participate in the good of self-integration, as I noted in Chapter 2, but also that they enable us to participate in all the other real goods in a distinctive way, too. Commitments enable us to *discover* what these genuine aspects of well-being are actually made of.

If we opt out of participating in particular goods when we experience adversity, when some aversive reaction arises, when appealing alternatives present themselves, when emotional fortitude fluctuates, or when we lose confidence in a project we've undertaken, we're not going to plumb the depths of the goods in which we participate.[20] Mere superficial engagement won't test or expand us or enable us fully and deeply to understand and embrace the various aspects of flourishing.

In order to participate deeply in any good, I need to take it seriously, and this will often mean devoting significant time, energy, and attention to it. I can *care* intensely about a good while only engaging with it briefly, of course, but I can't *participate in it* in a way that involves really coming to understand and experience it richly without, at least in many cases, engaging with it in a sustained and energetic way.[21] And I will need to approach the good with a certain measure of open-endedness, a willingness to explore, to respond flexibly in light of new discoveries and opportunities, and so forth. A friendship to which I commit on a three-month timeline will be one in which I am far less present than one to which I commit myself wholeheartedly. The same is true for a profession, an intellectual undertaking, or the development of a skill.

This obviously doesn't mean that, every time I participate in an aspect of well-being, I need to do so without qualification. Some commitments may be quite superficial and limited. But commitment makes it possible for me to embrace some goods intensively and extensively.

For a commitment to enable this kind of intensive and extensive embrace, I must uphold it even when I am disinclined to do so. It's not just, as in the context of one sort of purely instrumental approach to commitments, that I am seeking to realize what I anticipate will be my preferences in the future. Rather, I am shaping my priorities for the future *now*, giving participation in some goods precedence despite whatever my preferences might be at some relevant later date. I'm deciding that some preferences, at any rate, will trump ones I might acquire later that have the potential to conflict with them.

When I've chosen among many incommensurable goods, I can't claim that the option I've chosen is *the best* in any objective sense. The value of a particular good provides a perfectly good reason to choose it; but, acknowledging this value, I would still be perfectly free to choose other options instead. If I persist in adhering to this option, therefore, I need a reason for doing so that doesn't involve the mistaken belief that the values it embodies objectively outweigh those embodied by other options. The fact that I've committed provides just such a reason.

## B.  *Commitment and Planning*

We must make commitments because, in virtue of the incommensurability of the basic goods, we need to do so in order to establish priorities that equip us to plan rationally.

Because the basic aspects of well-being are incommensurable, there is, in general, no objective rank-ordering of states of affairs as objects of choice for me in abstraction from my choices. When I confront a range of possibilities, the goods involved in those possibilities do not ordinarily compel me to choose in just one way with respect to them. And this might be thought to place me in an impossible position, one in which I'm overwhelmed by vertigo as I confront an immense array of options.

Commitments serve to reduce the immense variety of options we confront to manageable size. They are especially crucial when we confront the possibility of making choices that concern large numbers of unpredictable events and uncertain feelings over the course of an extended future—the choice of a profession, a partner, a hobby, a region of residence, a religious community. By making commitments, we can establish priorities that enable us to allocate our time, energy, attention, and other resources to particular goods. As a general matter, there is no *a priori* reason to prefer one genuine aspect of well-being to another. But once I have made a commitment, I have given myself a reason, sometimes a decisive one, to do so subsequently.

We will frequently experience inclinations toward particular goods. And on a day-to-day basis many of our choices may reasonably be made simply by noting our inclinations and determining which potential actions we might undertake in response to them are consistent with the generic requirements of practical reasonableness. But preferences will not always be sufficient.

This is so not only because, as I have noted, we will not plumb the depths of particular goods without committing to them. It is also the case that we need to do so because our tangible and intangible resources are limited, and we will likely be unable to complete large-scale projects if we do not plan for them and assign them appropriate priorities. When we do this, we are able to formulate rational plans.

> If we have decided to build a highway through the desert, . . . we can use cost-benefit computations to select among materials and methods of leveling and road-building. But it was not, and could not rationally have been, cost-benefit computations which guided our prior commitment to the level of economic activity (trade) and personal mobility which calls for highways of this sort. We know that the building and use of highways of this sort involves the death of tens of thousands of persons, and the horrible injury of hundreds of thousands more, each year. But we have not made any computation which shows that the goods participated in and attained by that level of trade and mobility exceed, outweigh, are proportionately greater, than the goods destroyed and damaged by that level, or any level, of deaths and injuries. Nor, on the other hand, could any computation yield the conclusion that the deaths and injuries are an evil which objectively outweighs, exceeds, etc., the good of mobility, etc. . . . The justification, and equally the

critique, of any basic commitment must be in terms of the requirements of practical reasonableness, which give positive direction even though they do not include any principle of optimizing . . ., and even though they permit indefinitely many different commitments (as well as, also, excluding indefinitely many other possible commitments!).[22]

We will need to make commitments to particular projects. And we will sometimes need to make more comprehensive plans within which not only particular goods but also other plans find their places. It may sometimes even be the case that all one's plans will need to fit coherently together within an overall plan for one's life.[23]

If one embraces such a plan, it will surely rule out some commitments while making it essentially mandatory that one make and adhere to others. But the extent to which this is so will depend in large measure on whether one *has* an overall plan of life or not and, if so, how detailed it is. One will, as I have suggested already, have good reason to make commitments with respect to some goods. But it is less clear why one would necessarily fail to flourish if one declined to craft a relatively detailed and coherent plan of life.

The commitments one makes obviously need to be coherently realizable; it is unreasonable to make commitments that don't fit with one's other commitments, since doing so will have to mean relativizing or abandoning or altering one's commitments when one has no good reason to do so. And one likely has reason to make extensive commitments in some cases in order to experience the richness and depth of particular goods. But spontaneity and free self-creation will certainly matter in many cases, to many people, as well, and these can certainly be seen as aspects of the goods of practical reasonableness, play, and æsthetic experience (and perhaps also the good of knowledge, since a certain kind of discovery may be possible when there are fewer constraints on one's choices). Some lives will reasonably be structured with relative rigor, while others presumably will not. Where one has a comprehensive plan of life, it will place constraints on one's choices with respect to one's commitments, but one's plans will frequently be sufficiently open-ended that they will place only limited constraints on one's choices with respect to many of one's commitments. Nonetheless, one's commitments will need to be detailed enough to enable one to plan effectively for the future.

## IV. Commitments and Priorities

The understanding of incommensurability I have defended here has been criticized on the basis that, if basic aspects and instances of flourishing "cannot meaningfully be compared or weighed when engaging in practical reasoning,"[24] practical reasoning must be impossible or arbitrary. Recognizing the role played by commitments in enabling rational choice makes possible a response to this criticism. In fact, treating basic aspects of well-being as incommensurable is quite compatible with comparing or weighing these aspects of well-being. It's just that, when one is doing so, one isn't employing weights that just anyone would be unreasonable not to employ.

We clearly weigh categories of well-being, and individual instances of well-being, in the course of practical deliberation. We do so, however, *in light of our pre-existing commitments and preferences*. We are free to adopt a variety of commitments and to embrace a diverse array of preferences; but our having accepted particular preferences and commitments will constrain how we may reasonably choose with respect to the various goods we confront (as will such requirements as, say, that we pursue goods efficiently and that our commitments cohere with each other). What we cannot do, however, is claim that there is (at least ordinarily) anything rationally *required* about these commitments and preferences.

Critics of the kind of incommensurability thesis I defend here have offered a variety of examples designed to show that the belief that basic goods are incommensurable leads to counterintuitive consequences. Suppose, for instance, to use a case suggested by Jonathan Crowe, that my friend calls to ask for help as I'm watching a rerun of *Friends*. Intuitively, it seems as if there's no question that I should turn off the television and offer her assistance.[25] Does incommensurability imply that this is an open question? Similarly, on Jason Brennan's view,

> It seems rather obvious to me that a day spent marrying the love of my life better contributes to my overall flourishing or well-being than, say, a day spent watching a movie I slightly enjoy. It seems obvious that a prolonged and deep friendship with someone whom I love and with whom I share a mutual understanding better contributes to my well-being than a casual relationship with an office mate. It seems obvious that my guitar playing—a skill I have developed great capacity in over 23 years—better contributes to my well-being than my ability to play Super Mario Brothers 3 on occasion. It seems obvious that getting a tenure-track academic job at a prestigious university—something I worked hard to get for many years—is better than a day spent picking one's nose. On a collective level, it seems obvious that a world in which everyone is both virtuous and happy is better than a world in which everyone is in a pain amplifier.[26]

Brennan believes incommensurability has another counterintuitive implication.

> Now suppose you are a human being looking to flourish. How would you make rational decisions about what things to pursue? It seems all

you can do is put things into three categories—disvaluable, indifferent, and valuable. If you put more than one thing in the latter category and have to choose among them, you will pretty much have to flip a coin or role the dice. That is, if your goal is to flourish, and you have the choice between spending the day marrying the love of your life or picking your nose for fun, you are in the position of Buridan's ass. . . . So you might as well flip a coin.[27]

Obviously, it makes sense to value an actual friendship more highly than the experience of watching *Friends*. Meeting the needs of a close friend is certainly much higher on my preference scale, more supported by my commitments, than watching *Friends*—valuable though doing so is as an instance of æsthetic experience or imaginative immersion. But that my friend's claim objectively prevails will be a function of how it is appropriate for me to *choose* in the relevant situation in accordance with the requirements of practical reasonableness, and these requirements can dictate an outcome without any appeal to commensurability.

To understand someone as a friend is precisely (in part) to assign that person a high priority in one's deliberation. This will partly be a matter of any promises and less explicit undertakings one may have made verbally or by way of one's conduct. But it will also be a matter of integrating the other into my sense of who I am. And this, in turn, will be reflected not just in emotional reactions but also in my commitments (whether conscious or instinctive). I will necessarily, in making the relevant sorts of commitments, have assigned my friend a high priority in my life. If I hadn't committed myself in this way with respect to my friend, it would be odd to say that she was my friend at all. To treat her as my friend is, among other things, to judge (even if in a frequently indeterminate way) that her well-being is important. If I treated it as unimportant, I would not be treating her as a friend. And, given that she is a friend, and thus someone to whose well being I'm committed to assigning a high priority, the question of her importance admits of an obvious answer.

Thus, I don't need to think that the value of my friendship outweighs the value of the æsthetic experience involved in viewing *Friends* in any sort of impersonal fashion. I need only assume that *I* have assigned my friendship a higher weight, subjectively, in this case, as regards my own deliberation, in virtue of my commitment to this friendship (or, indeed, a commitment to friendship more generally); in virtue of thus assuming, I am committed to abandoning *Friends* in favor of my friend. So I can reach what Crowe rightly regards as the intuitively plausible result without making any general claims about the possibility of objectively weighing goods. I don't need to maintain that the values of friendship and *Friends* "are sufficiently comparable to say which should objectively prevail"[28] because I won't be reasoning in terms of the impersonal value of either but rather in terms of what practical reasonableness requires of me in this situation.

The same kind of point will apply in the case of Brennan's examples, including both the ones I noted earlier and the decision whether to spend the day "marrying the love of my life" or visiting "the Museum of Natural History—which I somewhat enjoy—for the twentieth time."[29] If someone is the love of my life, then that will mean having committed to treating her as central to my identity and my plans, so there will be no question of visiting the Museum of Natural History for the twentieth time as an alternative to spending a day joyously celebrating our relationship. Similarly, someone who has spent years learning the guitar will have reason to make choices with respect to guitar playing that she will not with respect to Super Mario Brothers 3—again, because of the role each is assigned by her commitments.

As I have noted, there are multiple requirements of practical reasonableness. They can reasonably be expected to narrow one's range of appropriate choices quite substantially. There are some ways in which you can and some ways in which you can't choose if your goal is to flourish. You will have good reason to take some paths rather than others. The incommensurability of goods does not leave you at loose ends. Ultimately, to be sure, you can choose freely among the options left open by practical reason. And, if you experience no emotional inclination toward one rather than another, it will, indeed, be perfectly reasonable for you to decide using some random procedure. But by the time you've reached the point at which this makes sense, you will have received significant help from the requirements of practical reasonableness in narrowing your choices. And it seems as if, once your choices have been narrowed in this way, there is no cause for regret if neither reason on its own nor reason in tandem with inclination succeeds in narrowing the available options to one and only one.

## V. The Possibility of Measurement

To say that the various aspects of well-being were commensurable would be to say that they could be measured on a common scale. This might mean that (*i*) they could all be measured using some sort of master good—either (*a*) a measurable substrate or essence underlying each good or (*b*) a value they contributed to bringing about and *in virtue* of bringing about which they mattered. Alternatively, it might mean that (*ii*) they could be meaningfully aggregated using some sort of objectively required weighting procedure. Commitment will play a role, though not an exclusive one, in helping to respond to concerns about the possibility of measuring basic aspects of well-being.

## A. *Commensuration and a Master Good*

If there were a master good of some kind, this could make it possible for the various aspects of well-being to be measured on a common scale. But there does not seem to be a master good of the needed variety.

To see how a master good could be used to enable us to commensurate various particular goods, imagine that what we're really seeking when we pursue this or that basic good is the *pleasure*—understood as some sort of conscious hedonic experience—embodied or produced by that good. It would be easy enough to substitute some other purported master good for pleasure. Now imagine that I am faced with two choices as regards a given evening's activity—to go to a concert alone or to play a game of squash with a friend. Ignoring issues of uncertainty about the future, suppose we say that my attendance at the concert will yield 12 units of æsthetic experience, while the game of squash will yield 90 units of play and 0.5 units of friendship.[30] Perhaps, the proponent of commensuration might suggest, 1 unit of æsthetic experience embodies or produces 1.5 units of pleasure—call them *hedons*; 1 unit of play embodies or produces 0.05 hedons, and 1 unit of friendship embodies or produces 25 hedons. In this case, we can say that attending the concert will yield 18 hedons and the game of squash 17 hedons. Thus, given that hedons are finally the only things that matter, it would be rational for me to prefer the movie to the quiet dinner.

While it might be convenient if there were, there don't seem to be any such things as hedons—measurable and qualitatively indistinguishable units of pleasure. Even when, as won't always be the case, they're sensorily indistinguishable, pleasures can be qualitatively differentiated by their objects, meanings, and contexts. So it doesn't look as if there are pleasures capable of playing the role needed for commensuration.

And, if there *were* hedons, they wouldn't be the only things that mattered. As I've already observed, we seem generally to understand the goods we seek to realize as inherently valuable. We don't treat them as worthwhile because they *produce* particular sensory experiences. Nor do we suppose that they are only valuable when they are *associated* with particular feelings. Friendship just isn't the same thing as, the experienced value of friendship doesn't lie in, some conscious pleasure or set of conscious pleasures. And the same will be true of any other discriminable psychological state that might be proposed in pleasure's place. (The exception, of course, is sensory pleasure sought for its own sake.) So it's not clear why we would have any special reason to seek to produce hedons. At best, hedons might be valuable *in addition* to all the other aspects of well-being, with which they would remain incommensurable; I would have no more reason to seek to produce or embody hedons than to seek to produce or realize any of the other goods. There would be no reason to think that the value of the other goods would be exhausted by their tendency to produce hedons. We would have no reason to treat the quantity of hedons produced by or realized in a given action as decisive vis-à-vis the choice to engage or not engage in that action. So, even if there were hedons, it's not clear why we could use the number of hedons realized in a particular state of affairs to compare that state of affairs as an object of choice with some other state of affairs.

I've focused on hedons for simplicity's sake. But the same reasons we might have to be skeptical about commensurating the various basic goods using hedons would apply were we to attempt to commensurate them using some other putative master good. The basic goods seem to be valuable for their own sakes and not for their tendency to produce or embody some other, distinguishable good. Any such good seems likely to be just another object of choice, not one that underlies or serves as the ultimate source of value for all the others, and thus incapable of serving as a basis for rational commensuration.

## B. *Commensuration and Generic Prudential Value?*

Perhaps the various aspects of well-being, while inherently and not only instrumentally valuable, and not reducible to some common substrate, can be aggregated using some sort of weighting procedure. James Griffin believes that we can employ this sort of procedure without an appeal to any master good.

Griffin argues that "[i]t is just a mistake to think that commensurability of prudential values needs a supreme substantive prudential value." Rather, he maintains, commensurability requires only "that 'prudential value' itself be a quantitative notion—that is, that it be able to figure in judgments as to 'more,' 'less,' or 'same' value, which it can."[31] In effect, Griffin thinks that it's possible to recognize all the particular goods we embrace, and to take them seriously as valuable on their own, while *also* supposing that there is a sort of generic prudential value, well-being, which can figure in both intrapersonal rational choice and in broadly consequentialist interpersonal calculations. Well-being, Griffin suggests, can be detected in our practices of making at least implicitly quantitative claims about our own and others' well-being.

Griffin does not offer us any reason to think that prudential value *could* be a quantitative notion, so it is hard to know how to respond to his blunt assertion. He maintains that "[t]he quantity used to define the scale of measurement of prudential value is not itself a substantive prudential value."[32] Since it is not a substantive value, it seems as if, absent some other pre-existing basis for commensuration, we will have no non-arbitrary basis for assigning the weights needed to create the kind of weighted sum Griffin envisions (apart from our own commitments, as I emphasized in Parts III and IV). And, if we can't generate prudential value in this way without arbitrariness, it doesn't seem as if there's anything maximizable that could *count* as prudential value.

Perhaps, as Griffin suggests in support of his contention that we treat well-being as quantifiable, we do sometimes use adjectives like "more" or "less" when we're talking about well-being in a general sense. But, if we do so, that we do is insufficient to show that there really is some unitary quantity in virtue of which we can engage in maximizing talk with regard to well-being. Sometimes it may be the case that our language here is simply in poor working order, that it embodies a significant error of some kind. But there is often, I think, a less disruptive explanation. The quantitative talk to which Griffin refers can be seen as a kind of shorthand. Sometimes, on this view, we use "more," "less," "better," "worse," and so forth to pick out not quantitative but rather qualitative distinctions between the potential objects of our choices that allow us to rank them.

Thus, while there is no way of ranking states of affairs quantitatively, there are several ways in which they can be ranked qualitatively. (*i*) A state of affairs involving no goods at all, if such a state of affairs is conceivable, would be inferior to one involving some good, any good. (*ii*) A state of affairs involving a given good will be outranked by one involving just the same good and one or more other goods. (*iii*) As an object of choice for me, a state of affairs that includes my acting reasonably is superior to a state of affairs in which I act unreasonably.[33] (The demands of reasonableness might rule out various possible choices with greater or lesser stringency.) But ranking in these ways does not require commensuration or maximization.[34] (Sometimes, of course, we *do* have quantitative distinctions in mind. But here we are engaged, not in global commensuration, but rather in commensuration in virtue of a scheme of priorities established by our commitments.)

Griffin defends his view not only by pointing to some of our linguistic practices but also by suggesting that we can at some points measure prudential value by measuring "the strength of informed desire."[35] However, (*i*) any behavioral evidence we offer for "the strength of informed desire" will of necessity be *post hoc*, and it will thus always be possible to interpret the evidence, not as evidence of some pre-existing desire supposed to *issue* in choice, but rather simply of the result of *having made* a choice. If I choose the symphony over a walk by the ocean, this does not show that there is any sense of desire in which my choosing the symphony can be *explained* with reference to the strength of my desire. Rather, to say that my desire to attend the symphony was stronger than my desire to walk by the ocean is simply to say that I chose to attend the symphony. Talk of strength of desire doesn't explain anything; it is simply a shorthand way of talking about what I actually choose. If I feel the pull of quite different alternatives and opt for one, that is no reason to suppose that I did so as the result of some sort of hydraulic process in accordance with which the force of one option's appeal simply overwhelms the force of the other's.[36] We do not necessarily decide in light of prior preference rankings, though we may not infrequently decide in light of schemes of priorities established by our commitments. Rather, our decisions, demonstrating preferences to which there is otherwise no objective access, serve to *constitute* our rankings (rankings which are rendered reasonable, or not, by our commitments).

In addition, (*ii*) even if informed desire could be ascertained and measured, this wouldn't help us measure well-being *itself*. As I have already suggested, well-being is a label for what is *worth* desiring. To measure desire mislocates the focus of deliberation from the desirable to the desirer's subjective state. I might desire some good or other very intensely, and, were measurement of my desire possible, its magnitude might tell us *something* about the value of what I desire (presuming I am adequately informed). Desire may be a proxy in some cases for the desirable. But it's not necessarily an especially good proxy.

Griffin also attempts to demonstrate that intrapersonal rational choice is possible by envisioning a variety of calculations involving trade-offs and probability estimates. He seeks to offer what is, in effect, a possibility proof: he suggests that we do, and therefore can, perform such calculations. And doubtless we do perform them on occasion. But, if the calculations are rational, if *we* are rational, we make them *within the terms* of our preferences and, especially, our antecedent commitments (as well as the more general requirements of practical reasonableness).[37] If I have already decided to, say, pursue a relationship with a particular lover, reason can exclude some means to this goal as inefficient and some actions (choosing to be a monk, dallying with another potential lover) as inconsistent with my objective. And practical reasonableness can rule out some prior choices on other grounds (*e.g.,* pursuing a lover obligated to be with someone else). It is within these sorts of constraints that I will evaluate my options. If I calculate and weigh possibilities among those left on the table, I will do so in light of the order of priorities established by my commitments. There is, indeed, "a place for cost-benefit analysis."[38] But that place is within the terms set by the requirements of practical reasonableness and by our commitments.

On Griffin's view, "the notion of 'quantity' of well-being" can be said to enter through ranking: quantitative differences are defined on qualitative ones. The quantity we are talking about is "prudential value," defined on informed rankings. All that we need for the all-encompassing scale is the possibility of ranking items on the basis of their nature. And we can, in fact, rank them in that way. We can work out trade-offs between different dimensions of pleasure or happiness. And when we do, we rank in a strong sense: not just choose one rather than the other, but regard it as worth more. That is the ultimate scale here: worth to one's life.[39]

But "worth to one's life" is not some objective quantity given apart from one's preferences and commitments. To be sure, something cannot be worthwhile for one's life if it is not the right sort of thing—if it is not an instance of or a means to a basic good. Many such goods are, however, available for one's embrace. Whether a given good is "worth more" is a function of one's preferences and, especially, one's commitments. And it is these preferences and commitments that make possible rankings and trade-offs for any given person.

It will make little sense to think of well-being as "prudential value" in Griffin's sense. Well-being is neither some master good instantiated in or underlying the various garden-variety goods we seek to realize, or worth-conferring because produced by those goods. But the alternative Griffin considers, in which we infer the existence of prudential value from our practices of desiring and ranking, arguably misconstrues what those practices at least often are and almost certainly misconstrues what they ought to be.

## VI. Incommensurability, Identity, and Priority

The various aspects of welfare present themselves as meriting our desire—as basic *goods*—and as not reducible to any substrate that might make it possible to commensurate them—as *basic* goods.

In light of our own experience of valuation, we might think that it made sense to regard valuation as a matter of responding rightly to features of our world (our experiences, activities, relationships, bodies) worth seeking because of their potential to constitute aspects of our own well-being. This is not a matter of realizing impersonal value without regard to its impingement on our own lives, but rather of seeking and realizing fulfillment, flourishing, in our own lives and those of others.

At first blush, we seem to experience the various aspects of well-being as irreducibly heterogeneous, and so as incommensurable. Griffin suggests that our practices of valuation and decision making make clear that commensuration of the sort needed for consequentialist calculation and similar strategies is perfectly possible. I have tried to show how these practices can be seen as intelligible without any appeal to commensuration and why proposals like Griffin's are unlikely to succeed. I believe, therefore, that we continue to have reason to acknowledge the incommensurability of the basic aspects of well-being.

If we do, this means, in turn, that we need to make commitments. We must do so, first of all, to participate in some of the basic goods, in some particular *instances* of these goods, in focused ways that allow us to plumb their depths. And we need to establish priorities that allow us to plan—and planning, of course, means investing in the relevant goods over time, rather than simply flitting from option to option. Making commitments for all the reasons I've noted means investing deeply and reminding ourselves repeatedly of the goods served by long-term self-involvement. To commit to participating in goods in this way shapes our identities and makes the goods we embrace our own, gives them priority claims on our loyalties and affections; and that it does helps to explain why belief in the incommensurability of basic goods need not have counterintuitive implications.

Recognizing the diversity of the incommensurable goods that present themselves for our choice prompts us to *make* commitments in order to realize some rather than others—and so creatively to shape our own identities—and to enable ourselves to plan rationally. It prompts us to *keep* commitments in order to preserve our identities and actually to plumb the goods we seek to realize. In shaping who we are, commitments—at least, the more extensive and intensive ones—may seem surprisingly similar to vocations, even though, at the same time, commitments and vocations might present themselves as phenomenologically rather different. I explore the relationship between the two in Chapter 4.

## Notes

1 *See* Timothy Chappell, Understanding Human Goods: A Theory of Ethics 37–45 (1995); Mark C. Murphy, Natural Law and Practical Rationality 96–138 (2001); 1 Germain Grisez, The Way of the Lord Jesus: Christian Moral Principles 121–25 (1983); John Finnis, Natural Law and Natural Rights 59–99 (1980).
2 *See* Murphy, *supra* note 1, at 46–48.
3 *See* Larry Arnhart, Darwinian Natural Right: The Biological Ethics of Human Nature 31–35 (1998); Donald Brown, Human Universals (1991); Morris Ginsberg, On the Diversity of Morals (1957).
4 The relevant sort of scrutiny can take various forms. We may identify something as a basic aspect of well-being in a variety of ways, including ascertaining whether (*i*) it seems to be a satisfactory terminus of desire; (*ii*) it is what seems at root to be harmed by what we would acknowledge unequivocally as an injury; (*iii*) it enjoys widespread cross-cultural recognition as sufficient to explain or justify a reasonable action; (*iv*) it survives scrutiny in Rawlsian reflective equilibrium; or (*v*) it could only be rejected as inherently valuable on pain of self-contradiction. *See, e.g.*, Grisez, *supra* note 1, at 122–23; Chappell, *supra* note 1, at 35–36; Murphy, *supra* note 1, at 40; Finnis, Law, *supra* note 1, at 81–90; John Rawls, A Theory of Justice 18–19, 42–45 (2d ed. 1999).
5 *See* John Finnis, Fundamentals of Ethics 38–41 (1983).

6 Except, of course, in the case of æsthetic experience and sensory pleasure, since having certain kinds of experiences is built into the definitions of these aspects of flourishing.

7 Thanks to David Gordon for comments on this topic.

8 On difficulties with various conative accounts of well-being, *see, e.g.*, RICHARD KRAUT, WHAT IS GOOD AND WHY: THE ETHICS OF WELL-BEING 66–130 (2007).

9 *Cf.* Owen J. Flanagan, Jr., *Quinean Ethics*, 93 ETHICS 56, 62 (1982).

10 *See* BERNARD WILLIAMS, *A Critique of Utilitarianism, in* UTILITARIANISM: FOR AND AGAINST 84–85 (J. J. C. Smart & Bernard Williams eds., 1973).

11 *See* ARNHART, *supra* note 3, at 31–35; BROWN, *supra* note 3; GINSBERG, *supra* note 3.

12 I thus agree with Jason Brennan that "to say that something is valuable is just a roundabout way of saying that we have reason to respond to it in certain ways and to act in certain ways toward it." Jason Brennan, *Controversial Ethics as a Foundation for Controversial Political Theory*, 7 STUD. EMERGENT ORDER 299, 305 (2014). There is nothing more interesting to say about well-being, fulfillment, or flourishing than this.

13 OWEN FLANAGAN, *Ethics Naturalized: Ethics as Human Ecology, in* MIND AND MORALS: ESSAYS IN COGNITIVE SCIENCE AND ETHICS 22 (Larry May et al. eds., 1996).

14 Williams, *Critique, supra* note 10, at 145.

15 *Id.* at 80.

16 *Id.* The only alternative Williams considers is that happiness might be understood as a discriminable psychological state.

17 *Id.* at 144. Williams adds, "and they may not be private," but this seems to take us in another direction.

18 *Id.* at 80.

19 On these justifications for making and keeping commitments, *see* Germain Grisez, *Against Consequentialism*, 23 AM. J. JURIS 21, 38–39, 60, 69, 72 (1978); GERMAIN GRISEZ & RUSSELL SHAW, BEYOND THE NEW MORALITY: THE RESPONSIBILITIES OF FREEDOM 45–50, 113, 124, 233–36 (3d ed. 1988); FINNIS, LAW, *supra* note 1, at 109–10; FINNIS, ETHICS, *supra* note 5, at 90; GERMAIN GRISEZ, *A Contemporary Natural-Law Ethics, in* MORAL PHILOSOPHY: HISTORICAL AND CONTEMPORARY ESSAYS 125, 136–37 (William C. Starr & Richard C. Taylor eds., 1989); GRISEZ, *supra* note 1, at 236–38. Grisez uses "commitments" to refer to the members of a limited subclass of the choices on which I'm focusing here: he's concerned especially with choices that are quite extensive and open-ended.

20 *See* NEIL STRAUSS, THE GAME: INSIDE THE SECRET WORLD OF PICKUP ARTISTS 169 (2008).

21 Thanks to David Gordon for comments on this point.

22 FINNIS, ETHICS, *supra* note 5, at 91–92; *cf. id.* at 90.

23 *See, e.g.*, MURPHY, *supra* note 1, at 210; FINNIS, LAW, *supra* note 1, at 103–05.

24 Jonathan Crowe, *Natural Law Anarchism*, 7 STUD. EMERGENT ORDER 288, 291 (2014).

25 *See id.* at 291–92.

26 Brennan, *supra* note 12, at 302.

27 *Id.* at 305.

28 Crowe, *supra* note 24, at 291. In addition, it would be wrong in virtue of the Principle of Fairness for me to ignore her need for immediate assistance. This principle dictates that I not discriminate arbitrarily among those affected by my

actions. Because I would not be willing that my friend ignore my urgent need in order to watch an episode of *Friends*, it would be unreasonable of me, because inconsistent, to ignore her urgent need to watch an episode of *Friends*.

29 Brennan, *supra* note 12, at 305.

30 Individual instances of basic aspects of well-being are, as I've noted, non-fungible, but I ignore this point here for simplicity's sake.

31 JAMES GRIFFIN, VALUE JUDGMENT: IMPROVING OUR ETHICAL BELIEFS 149 n.18 (1996). *Cf.* JAMES GRIFFIN, *Incommensurability: What's the Problem?*, *in* INCOMMENSURABILITY, INCOMPARABILITY, AND PRACTICAL REASON 35, 36, 262 nn.5–7 (Ruth Chang ed., 1997).

32 GRIFFIN, JUDGMENT, *supra* note 31, at 90.

33 For all I have argued, other sorts of qualitative comparisons among states of affairs might be possible. It might the case, for instance, that one sort of good was always objectively better than another. But it is not obvious that this would be of much benefit to the proponent of any position dependent on the possibility of commensurating the values of various options and ranking them accordingly. Thanks to David Gordon for this point.

34 *See* FINNIS, ETHICS, *supra* note 5, at 90–94.

35 JAMES GRIFFIN, WELL BEING: ITS MEANING, MEASUREMENT AND MORAL IMPORTANCE 99 (1986).

36 The notion that talk about the strength of desire is only an oversimplified way of referring *post hoc* to what we in fact do rather than any sort of *explanation* of our actions is, of course, controversial. There are arguments worth taking seriously for the view that we are not limited to "demonstrated" or "revealed" preferences. I hope the reader will pardon me for not wandering into this particular sticky wicket here.

37 Perhaps if I choose to make a preference the basis for the sort of calculation needed to conduct a cost-benefit analysis I am in so doing making a commitment; perhaps the distinction between commitments and mere preferences breaks down at this point.

38 *See* David Schmidtz, *A Place for Cost-Benefit Analysis*, 35 NOÛS 148 (2001).

39 GRIFFIN, WELL BEING, *supra* note 35, at 99.

# 4    Commitment and Vocation

*Commitments and vocations turn out to be much more alike than we might first suppose, and there may be good reason to rethink vocations as particularly pressing situational invitations to commitment.*

## I.  Identity, Focus, Commitment, and Vocation

Particularly when they are deep and wide-ranging, commitments can serve to shape our identities. They make particular goods, particular aspects of well-being, *ours*. In this respect, they are interestingly like vocations—even though in another way the two phenomena are interestingly different. I begin in Part II by examining the idea of vocation before going on in Part III to consider some alternative potential grounds for vocations. Then, while acknowledging the superficial differences between the two ideas, I suggest in Part IV that there may be more overlap between them than we might expect. I sum up in Part V.[1]

## II.  The Idea of Vocation

Vocations and commitments seem to play similar roles in people's lives. Out of a vast array of available goods, a vocation makes some *mine*. A commitment can do the same thing. However, making a commitment seems to be an exercise in self-creation, while a vocation seems to be something one *accepts*.

We often use the word "vocation" as an uninformative synonym for "job." But of course the term has a richer and more interesting range of meaning. A vocation in the broad sense is a task one is *called* (the root of "vocation" suggests an association with "calling") to assume. In Catholicism, a vocation is understood especially as a divine call to the priesthood, so that people concerned that there aren't more priests-in-training will lament a "decline in vocations." In Luther's version of Protestantism, the idea of vocation was understood very broadly, so that one could view work of any (morally licit) variety as the product of a divine calling. And in contemporary moral thought, both religious and secular, the idea of vocation is sometimes treated even more broadly, in such a way that any set of important, identity-constitutive responsibilities, whether or not related to work, might be understood as vocational.[2] One might be presented with these responsibilities as a demand or as an invitation.[3]

So, for instance, Larry Blum suggests that André Trocmé, the Protestant pastor who spearheaded the hiding and protection of Jewish children at Le Chambon in France during World War II, had a vocation that was not necessarily shared by church members who participated in his efforts.[4] And Robert Adams proposes that we think of Dietrich Bonhoeffer as having had a vocation to care about and participate in life in his native Germany, a vocation in virtue of which he left New York, where he was visiting on a fellowship at Union Theological Seminary, in order to go home and confront the growing darkness there, even at great personal cost.[5]

But a vocation might have a less dramatic flavor. Imagine for instance that Avery, a writer, discovers over time a deep kinship with and fascination at the work of Taylor, a deceased maker of independent films whom Avery has never met. More and more, the sense, *I need to give Taylor voice; I need to ensure that Taylor's forgotten creativity is discovered and appreciated, whether or not I'm personally recognized for performing this work of recovery*, presses in on Avery's consciousness. Avery might in such a case commit to bringing Taylor's work to public attention. But the commitment might seem to flow from the sense of being *called*, the sense that writing about Taylor is a task that has been *given* to Avery.

Phenomenologically, a vocation seems to come from *outside*—whether as a demand or as an invitation. It doesn't present itself as something *chosen*. At the same time, however, it also seems to come from *inside*—insofar as it doesn't feel like an alien imposition, but rather as something that fits with who one is, something that's a natural, even if not inevitable, expression of one's identity. It won't ordinarily appear just to fit with one's identity, given that I can reshape that identity; nonetheless, when it is discerned, it will seem consonant with whom one is at a deep level.

## III. Grounding Vocation

Possible grounds for the idea of vocation—in divine commands, in a non-consequentialist notion of optimality, in singular situational demands, or in consequentialism—all seem problematic.

### A. *Vocation and Theistic Voluntarism*

In traditional terms, a vocation has been seen as a product of the divine will. On this view, *God calls* someone to be a priest, or a cobbler, or to write about Taylor. The implication is that God has *selected* a particular task or opportunity for me. But this seems to be a problematic notion for more than one reason.

Crucially, it falls foul of difficulties that seem to attend divine command theories of ethics generally.[6] (*i*) If it's already clear how I need to reason about action and choose in order to flourish (and to attend appropriately to the flourishing of others), then a divine command seems superfluous. (*ii*) If what is to count as my well-being is itself a function of what God commands (not all divine command views would say that it was), then talk about divine love becomes meaningless, since to say that God seeks my well-being will be compatible with God's doing anything at all. (*iii*) If a divine command simply tracks a pre-existing moral requirement, it's unnecessary; but if it doesn't, if it imposes a new requirement that doesn't flow from the existing requirements of practical reasonableness, then it seems as if it's an arbitrary imposition, a subjection of the one receiving the command to an arbitrary will. This will be true even if a divine vocation selects one reasonable form of flourishing or fulfillment for an agent in preference to others, since excluding these others—which are, *ex hypothesi*, reasonable— would seem to be arbitrary and coercive. It seems difficult to square issuing option-restricting divine commands with divine regard for human freedom or with divine goodness or love more generally. Put more bluntly, a vocation that was effected by a divine command seems likely to be oppressive.[7]

### B. *Vocation, Natural Law, and Optimality*

Germain Grisez attempts to defend a conception of vocation consistent with natural law theory, which is ordinarily viewed as rooting moral requirements in human flourishing rather than the divine will. Central to the idea of vocation as he articulates it is a notion of optimization that is not obviously consistent with this theoretical framework.[8]

Natural law theory is incompatible with theistic voluntarism.[9] While Grisez and the other principal natural law theorists are theists, their conception of human welfare and of practical reasonableness makes right action a matter of participation in authentic aspects of well-being through rational action. Either a given action is consistent with the requirements of practical reasonableness or it is not. And if an action otherwise is consistent with the requirements of practical reasonableness, then it is unclear what sort of reason a divine vocation might be thought to give one for not performing it.

Grisez attempts to respond to this challenge by maintaining that [n]ot all possibilities are equally good. As a loving Father, God prefers that we choose the best. If we always did that, we would make the best use of our abilities, take advantage of the greatest opportunities, and benefit others and ourselves as richly as possible. And, as with other good choices, we also would meet the most serious threats and challenges and care for others and ourselves as effectively as we could.[10]

God "will guide each of us personally to *what is best* for us and everyone else."[11]

It seems at least difficult to square with natural law theory the notion that there is, in general, a "best possibility" in a given situation, unless we use "best" simply to refer to the range of possibilities consistent with the requirements of practical reasonableness. For the natural law rejection of consequentialism depends in part precisely on the recognition that the notion of a best possible state of affairs is incoherent and that quantitative rankings of states of affairs in general are impossible. Reasonable actions will pursue and realize diverse, incommensurable goods in varied ways that do not admit of rank-ordering. It is difficult to affirm a conception of vocation as the choice of the best in tandem with the reminder that "the glory of God may . . . be manifested in *any* of the many aspects of human flourishing" and that "love of God may . . . thus take, and be expressed in, any of the inexhaustibly many life-plans which conform to the requirements" of practical reason.[12]

Perhaps Grisez might have in mind a sense of "best possibility" in virtue of which the relevant possibility is *qualitatively* superior to the alternatives. If this possibility is qualitatively superior in virtue of the principles of practical reasonableness, it will be superior because other options are inconsistent with those principles (or because it involves all the goods embodied in some other possibility *plus* others).[13] But the requirements of practical reasonableness are unlikely to leave just one option on the table: they will filter out some options, but probably not all. Once unreasonable options have been ruled out, the diversity of goods embodied in the remaining reasonable options and actualized in and through choices for those options will, it seems, preclude rank-ordering them.

Alternatively, suppose the putative qualitative superiority of an option is *not* a function of its being unlike other possibilities in having not been ruled out by the principles of practical reasonableness. In this case, the question will be why this option should be regarded as an instance of qualitative *superiority* rather than as an instance of qualitative *difference*. In particular, if some sort of free divine choice is putatively the source of the qualitative difference, we will want to know both why making such a choice shouldn't be thought to be oppressive and arbitrary and why, given that it is not a function of well-being, it ought to play a significant role in the decision making of the finite agent in question.

There is the further complication that, on Grisez's view, no one *does wrong* by ignoring her personal vocation.[14] If this is the case, then declining to reason with reference to one's vocation in a particular case presumably does no wrong, either (presuming she hasn't made a binding commitment to following the putative vocation—a commitment not, among other things, predicated on the incorrect belief that the vocation would bind absent the commitment).

There is good reason to be thoroughly critical of the "secret, often unconscious legalism" of consequentialism, of "its assumption that there is a uniquely correct moral answer (or specifiable set of correct moral answers) to all genuine moral problems."[15] A natural law view contrasts starkly with consequentialism in virtue of its recognition that there is rarely a single best option for an agent to embrace. It seems most unlikely that an overall life-plan, the central elements of which are chosen in accordance with the principles of practical reasonableness, could be said to be better or worse than another such life-plan, given the incommensurability of the basic aspects of well-being. Given that it is impossible to rank-order options quantitatively on any objective basis, and that qualitative rank-ordering will generally leave multiple possibilities on the table, the notion of personal vocation as a call to realize the best option seems problematic.

## C. Vocation and Consequentialism

There are, of course, other ways of thinking about vocations. In particular, a vocation might flow from non-arbitrary moral requirements, whether general or particular. Act-consequentialism, for instance seems frequently likely in principle to yield very specific situational requirements, since what maximizes good consequences in a given case will vary from circumstance to circumstance.[16] To be sure, act-consequentialism is difficult to square with the moral weight of a vocation as it's often experienced, given that a vocation doesn't normally obtain simply in a limited situation, but instead seems to apply over an extended period—the period required to live out one's role as a monk, or write a book about a neglected filmmaker. Act-consequentialism seems unlikely to support the stability of character needed for this kind of self-investment: act-consequentialist vocations seem unlikely to exhibit persistent stability, since circumstances continue to alter and what will be needed to maximize good consequences will thus change with them, potentially moment by moment.[17] And of course, in any case, there are multiple reasons to be skeptical about consequentialism of any sort.[18]

## D. Vocation, Particularism, and the Call of the Other

Many moral theories other than act-consequentialism leave, and are valued by their advocates as leaving, considerable room for creative self-development, so that most of the time one will not confront richly situation-specific requirements. But of course some theories, even though generally permissive, might in some specific situations entail the adoption of very particular paths. Still, these theories will apply to everyone similarly situated in a relatively generic way; and perhaps it is part of the phenomenology of vocation that a vocation is uniquely individual, that it expresses and responds to the particularity of someone's character, personality, and circumstances.

One alternative that could, by contrast, account for the specificity of a vocation without appealing to divine commands is full-blown moral particularism.[19] The particularist holds that all of the factors that obtain in a given situation are germane to the question of how an agent ought to behave in that situation. These factors acquire their situation-specific moral salience in relation to each other, so that moral judgments appropriate in a given situation can't be identified in generic terms, since generic specification of the relevant factors will leave out potentially relevant situational variables.

If particularism proved correct, one could certainly confront very distinctive individual requirements unlike or in addition to those we might ordinarily expect. And it would, I suppose, be a situation- and agent-specific matter whether relevant requirements could continue to obtain over an extended period, as they are often experienced as doing in connection with vocations.

Particularism can explain, then, how a vocation might be binding on the recipient without any sort of generalization regarding the requirements faced by others. This is, of course, a reflection of how particularism works in general. I think that, despite the initial appeal of particularism, human situations do exhibit morally relevant generic features in ways that make patterned practical reasoning of the kind defended in NCNL theory quite defensible. Whatever else obtains in a situation in which someone decides purposefully to attack noncombatants, for instance, there is this: *the purpose to attack noncombatants*. And my instinct is that a good case can be made for the view that acting on this purpose will always be unreasonable, whatever one's circumstances; this purpose will always be salient in a decisively relevant way. But of course the particularist may turn out to be able to respond effectively to this challenge.

The kind of moral approach associated with a certain sort of Continental postmodernism might similarly capture the phenomenology of vocation without any appeal to arbitrary divine commands. This sort of approach focuses on the singular encounter with the other—and, particularly, the face of other, as generating an inescapable sense of demand.[20] It could, in principle, involve a recognition of the requisite sort of vulnerability in the face of Taylor, the filmmaker, say. This sort of approach is similar to particularism in that it's thoroughly situation-specific, but it might differ both in the focus specifically on the face of the other and in its attention to the demand exerted by that face (in contrast with what might turn out to be a broader range of moral experiences captured by particularism).

This sort of Continental approach is interestingly appealing. But one might wonder whether it doesn't encounter the same difficulties as particularism does when it comes to generic features of reality that might prove morally salient. In addition, while particularism features a general theoretical account (even if one by which I'm unpersuaded) of why we might expect situations to be morally singular, the similar Continental approach does seem more compatible, in principle, with a recognition of generic situational features, if only because it doesn't offer a general theoretical account positively supportive of situational singularity. One might think, in any case, that good arguments for specific views responsive to generic features of reality—like the NCNL view—might show that those views could withstand the challenge of a Continental quasi-particularism centered on the face. One might think, further, that a more systematic view, whether concerned with virtues or principles, might be able to explain the phenomenology of moral experience to which the Continental approach appeals. Finally, one might wonder whether a moral approach that focuses just on the other is as effectively equipped to capture the richness of moral experience, inclusive of concern with self and other alike and often declining to see the interests of the two as radically opposed, as alternative principle-and virtue-based approaches.

One thing to note is that, for both particularism and the Continental approach I have described, a vocation will simply be a particular instance of obligation generally. The kind of experience that gives rise to what we might think of as a vocational obligation will be the kind of experience that births every obligation we have. What will distinguish vocational from other obligations in this case will thus be not their particularity but, rather, their comprehensiveness and their engagement with the identities of those to whom they are presented. But this will be, it seems, a matter of degrees.

## IV. Commitment and Vocation: Convergence?

Vocations and commitments occupy the same general moral terrain, since both help to link us with particular goods in ways that general moral principles don't, to the same degree or in the same way. But they appear to do so in different ways. Even if we can't immediately articulate a clear grounding for vocation, even if vocations and commitments are alike in helping to provide us with moral focus, even if both are relevant to our identities, it still seems as if there are important differences between the two. I might, as I've noted, commit to fulfilling a vocation. But a vocation will at least often *feel* as if it has moral weight *before* I commit, as if I *ought* to commit to it. Indeed, when I commit to following a vocation that presents itself as a demand, the commitment is normatively superfluous: it doesn't add any extra duties to my portfolio, just like a commitment to, say, avoiding purposeful attacks on noncombatants.

But perhaps the distinctions, even if real, are less pronounced than might initially appear to be the case. On the one hand, as I have already noted, a vocation may present itself as an invitation, an opportunity: it may urge consideration of a possibility rather than embodying an inescapable demand.[21] A vocation in this sense would be and seem strongly *appealing* without also seeming *obligatory*. And in response to *this* sort of vocation, one could, indeed, make a commitment that would involve the active embrace of the vocation and that would give the vocation new moral weight. Since one wouldn't be required to fulfill the vocation, doing so would be optional absent the commitment, but one could make fulfilling the vocation in some sense required (at least to some degree) by making the commitment.

What would it mean in this case for the vocation to be strongly attractive? Presumably that it touched one's own desires, identity, capacities, and circumstances in a central way. Consider Avery again. Delighting in Taylor's personality and work, Avery might be excited by the prospect of sharing Taylor's story out of concern for Taylor and Taylor's own legacy. Avery might also relish the transformative potential of the work and want to share it with others for that reason, too. And Avery might see the prospect of writing about Taylor, of making Taylor's work comprehensible and appealing to others, as an intellectual and literary challenge, and as an opportunity to grow as a writer and speaker and interpreter of culture and to build new connections within the world of film scholarship and criticism and with the film-appreciating public. For all these reasons, Avery might actively desire to write about Taylor. In addition, the prospect of writing about Taylor might engage Avery's own identity. Avery might feel empathically connected with Taylor. Writing about Taylor might express and fulfill Avery's existing self-understanding as a writer and scholar. And a sense of the kind of life embracing and completing the project of telling Taylor's story could make possible might prove compellingly appealing to Avery. Avery's capacities and background would obviously be relevant as well—factors including Avery's education, experience as a writer about the film scene, knowledge of intellectual and cultural history, and ability to tell stories and to interpret cultural products might all make this an especially attractive option. And Avery's circumstances might play a part, too: a geographic location near key archival materials, connections with people in the film world who could help with the project, acquaintance with Taylor's family members, a work schedule less likely to interfere with the work than some others', and the absence of conflicting family obligations might all help to increase the fit between Avery and the project of telling Taylor's story.

But notice that this array of factors needn't be understood in relation to particularism about moral requirements, or divine commands, or consequentialism to play an important role here. While these can be cashed as conveying the invitation to accept a vocation, a vocation that would become binding on acceptance, they could also be understood as proposing a commitment that would then, again, create obligations once made.

Indeed, other requirements of practical reasonableness, like the Principle of Fairness, might, perhaps in tandem with other principles and prior commitments and the sorts of factors I've talked about in Avery's case, make it unreasonable not to embrace certain commitments. Thus, while a vocation understood as an invitation might indeed be optional, just like a typical commitment, some sorts of commitments might sometimes present themselves as at least close to inescapable, not unlike the paradigmatic vocation.

In addition, while preserving one's identity might not be sufficient to generate obligations (at least apart from Williams-style ground projects), identity preservation might provide strong, appealing reasons to make a commitment (to, say, writing about Taylor). That the view I am developing here can take this sort of consideration into account will provide further reason to see the gap between commitments as I'm envisioning them and vocations as commonly understood as very narrow indeed.

## V. The Narrow Gap Between Commitment and Vocation

We need not accept theistic voluntarism to embrace the idea of vocation. Particularism or the Continental focus on the face of the other (or even consequentialism) might do the trick. But, even if we're skeptical about particularism (or consequentialism), we might nonetheless think that something like the understanding of commitment (and of ethics more generally) on which I have focused might capture much or all of the phenomenology of vocation—both vocation as invitation and vocation as demand. Similarly, the notion of a vocation as an invitation might both narrow the distance between vocational and commitment-based obligations considerably and also relieve the idea of vocation of much that we might find troubling about it—as a kind of arbitrary imposition. This will be true particularly if the invitation is a matter of the receiver's desires, identity, capacities, and circumstances.

What someone is offered in a vocation will often, perhaps always, be an opportunity to *love* deeply and determinedly.[22] Commitments and vocations alike serve to channel, deepen, and support our loves. In Chapter 5, I explore the role of commitment in enabling and sustaining one crucial variety of love.

# Notes

1 Thanks to Tanja M. Laden for a conversation about vocation and commitment that prompted the formulation of the ideas I've expressed in this chapter.

2 The best discussions by philosophers of the idea of vocation of which I'm aware are: ROBERT MERRIHEW ADAMS, *Vocation, in* FINITE AND INFINITE GOODS: A FRAME-WORK FOR ETHICS 292, 292–317 (1999); KEITH WARD, *Vocation, in* ETHICS AND CHRISTIANITY 141, 141–54 (1970); LAWRENCE A. BLUM, MORAL PERCEPTION AND PARTICULARITY 104–23, 167–69 (1994); GERMAIN GRISEZ & RUSSELL SHAW, PERSONAL VOCATION (2003); DAVID L. NORTON, *Education for Self-Knowledge and Worthy Living, in* ETHICAL ISSUES IN CONTEMPORARY SOCIETY 155 (John Howie & George Schedler eds., 1994). *Cf.* DAVID L. NORTON, PERSONAL DESTINIES: A PHILOSOPHY OF ETHICAL INDIVIDUALISM (1976).

3 On vocation as invitation, *see* ADAMS, *supra* note 2, at 303.

4 *See* BLUM, *supra* note 2, at 167 n.26.

5 *See* ADAMS, *supra* note 2, at 293–94, 296–97.

6 *See, e.g.,* GARY CHARTIER, THE ANALOGY OF LOVE 151–63 (2d ed. 2017).

7 Thanks to David Gordon for discussion on this point.

8 In my discussion of Grisez's position, I incorporate, with modifications, a small amount of material from an earlier book: *see* GARY CHARTIER, ECONOMIC JUSTICE AND NATURAL LAW 61–64 (2009).

9 *See, e.g.,* 1 GERMAIN GRISEZ, THE WAY OF THE LORD JESUS: CHRISTIAN MORAL PRINCIPLES 101–02 (1983); JOHN FINNIS, NATURAL LAW AND NATURAL RIGHTS 342–43, 406–07, 410 (1980).

10 GRISEZ & SHAW, VOCATION, *supra* note 2, at 10.

11 *Id.* at 11 (my italics).

12 FINNIS, LAW, *supra* note 9, at 113.

13 *See* Chapter 3.V.B, *supra.*

14 *See* GRISEZ & SHAW, VOCATION, *supra* note 2, at 10.

15 JOHN FINNIS, FUNDAMENTALS OF ETHICS 93 (1983).

16 *See* ADAMS, *supra* note 2, at 297–300 (discussing a possible consequentialist account of vocation).

17 *Cf.* J. J. C. Smart, *An Outline of a System of Utilitarian Ethics, in* UTILITARIAN-ISM: FOR AND AGAINST 1, 9–12 (J. J. C. SMART & BERNARD WILLIAMS eds.,1973), agreeing, from an act-utilitarian standpoint, "that an adequate rule-utilitarianism would not only be extensionally equivalent to the act-utilitarian principle . . . but would in fact consist of one rule only, the act-utilitarian one." *Id.* at 11–12.

18 *See, e.g.,* Stephen R. L. Clark, *Natural Integrity and Biotechnology, in* HUMAN LIVES 58 (Jacqueline A. Laing & David S. Oderberg eds., 1997); ALAN DONAGAN, THE THEORY OF MORALITY 172–209 (1977); FINNIS, ETHICS, *supra* note 15, at 80–108; FINNIS, LAW, *supra* note 9, at 111–19; JOHN M. FINNIS ET AL., NUCLEAR DETERRENCE, MORALITY, AND REALISM 177–296 (1987); GERMAIN G. GRISEZ & RUSSELL SHAW, BEYOND THE NEW MORALITY: THE RESPONSIBILITIES OF FREEDOM 111–14, 131–33 (3d ed. 1988); ALASDAIR C. MACINTYRE, AFTER VIRTUE: A STUDY IN MORAL THEORY 61–63, 67–68, 185 (2d ed. 1984); NEL NODDINGS, CARING: A FEMININE APPROACH TO ETHICS & MORAL EDUCATION 151–54 (1984); DAVID S. ODERBERG, MORAL THEORY: A NON-CONSEQUENTIALIST APPROACH 65–76, 97–101, 132–33 (2000); BERNARD WILLIAMS, MORALITY: AN INTRODUCTION TO ETHICS (2d ed. 1993); BERNARD WILLIAMS, *A Critique of Utilitarianism, in* SMART & WILLIAMS, *supra* note 17, at 77–150; Germain Grisez, *Against Consequentialism*, 23 AM. J. JURIS 21 (1978).

19 The standard discussions of particularism are JONATHAN DANCY, MORAL REASONS (1993) and JONATHAN DANCY, ETHICS WITHOUT PRINCIPLES (2004). Keith Ward rejects theistic voluntarism while defending a very situation-specific conception of vocation; *see* WARD, *supra* note 2, at 141–45. This suggests that his underlying account of morality might be worked out in particularist terms, though he insists that we should see the example of Jesus as decisive even as we recognize that it may not be appropriate to seek to embody that example in any direct way in many particular circumstances.

20 *See* EMMANUEL LEVINAS, *Substitution, in* THE LEVINAS READER 88 (Seán Hand ed., 1989); KNUD LØGSTRUP, THE ETHICAL DEMAND (1997); ZYGMUNT BAUMAN, POSTMODERN ETHICS (1993); ZYGMUNT BAUMAN, LIFE IN FRAGMENTS: ESSAYS IN POSTMODERN MORALITY (1995); ZYGMUNT BAUMAN, MORTALITY, IMMORTALITY AND OTHER LIFE STRATEGIES 200–10 (1992); JOHN D. CAPUTO, AGAINST ETHICS: CONTRIBUTION TO A POETICS OF OBLIGATION WITH CONSTANT REFERENCE TO DECON-STRUCTION (1993); JOHN D. CAPUTO, DEMYTHOLOGIZING HEIDEGGER (1993); EDITH WYSCHOGROD, SAINTS AND POSTMODERNISM: REVISIONING MORAL PHILOSOPHY (1990); ROBERT GIBBS, WHY ETHICS? SIGNS OF RESPONSIBILITIES (2000). *Cf.* IRIS MURDOCH, THE SOVEREIGNTY OF GOOD (1970); DWIGHT FURROW, AGAINST THEORY: CONTINENTAL AND ANALYTIC CHALLENGES IN MORAL PHILOSOPHY (1995); WENDY M. FARLEY, EROS FOR THE OTHER: RETAINING TRUTH IN A PLURALISTIC WORLD (1995).

21 *See* ADAMS, *supra* note 2, at 303.

22 I owe this idea to Robert Adams.

# 5  Commitment and Love

*Love is an investment of the self, a commitment, and commitments of various kinds help to realize and sustain loving relationships.*

## I.  Love Commits

There are multiple, overlapping general reasons for making commitments and keeping them. But we should also expect there to be reasons specific to the goods internal to individual practices and domains for making and keeping commitments in support of those practices and within those domains. In this chapter, I want to examine the role of commitments in enacting and supporting interpersonal erotic love. I presuppose what I've already noted about the general reasons for making and keeping commitments, though I will at points advert to my earlier discussions. But I will also note a number of specific rationales for making and keeping commitments that are especially relevant to this context.[1] This discussion of commitment and love will prove useful on its own, I trust, as well as illustrating and clarifying what I've said up to this point regarding the nature and significance of commitments.

I begin with a brief sketch of the nature and initial dynamics of love (Part II). I go on to discuss a range of ways in which commitment is generally relevant throughout love's trajectory (Part III). In addition to these ways, germane to love at all its stages, I examine specific roles played by commitment in particular stages: during the process of wooing the beloved (Part IV), of reconstituting a relationship with the beloved after a breakup (Part V), and of deepening and extending and preserving love in the context of permanent partnership (Part VI), before concluding with a brief overview (Part VII).

## II.  The Beginning of Love

We often focus on one sort of commitment in love: the mutual commitment to forming a self-conscious *we*. When we talk about a "committed relationship," this is usually what we have in mind. But in this case we're concerned with the *promissory* grounds of the relationship. Promises matter a great deal to love; indeed, they do so well before marital promises are exchanged. But I want to note the significance of commitments in my sense—of firm decisions, resolutions, that are distinct from, even if they also complement and serve to support, promises—for love. In Part II, I want to lay the groundwork for what I will go on to say about the role of commitment in love by sketching love's origins and initial dynamics.

## A.  Love and Choice

Love is a chosen disposition of the self, a decision,[2] the will to form a *we* with the other, to identify with the other, to define oneself in part in relation to the other.

This opening of myself to the other—so that she now becomes not just *the other* but also *the beloved*—may on its own amount to nothing more than a momentary choice.[3] But it may sometimes be not merely a momentary movement of will but actually a commitment that stretches into the future. "Real love has its will to endure built right in-to it. . . . Love, like all emotions, is a product of the will, and in the willfulness of love the idea of fleeting romance is all but unthinkable."[4] One may choose not merely to love *now* but to project one's love forward in time. One may choose for one's future as well as for one's present. And in this case one's choice has become a commitment.

## B.  Reasons and Occasions for Committing to Love

Love is proposed by what I call the evocative impulses—delight, desire, care, attachment,[5] friendship. These impulses respond to and highlight appealing features of the other, both his characteristics *in se* and relevant features of his relationships with the potential lover and with others. The evocative impulses may arise in us relatively unbidden, though of course each of them can and almost certainly will be nurtured by our choices. But whether I will open myself to loving the other *in light of* these impulses, whether I will love, is finally up to me.

So, prompted by the evocative impulses, one's heart goes out to the other. One prizes the other and one's relationship with him (whether it has already begun or presents itself only as a prospect). And one elects to give him and one's relationship with him (if and when it begins) pride of place in one's personal hierarchy of values. One might respond in such a case to the other's sense of wonder, his passion for a cause, his physical beauty, his penchant for whimsy, or any number of other factors. And one might, in fact, respond not so much to any particular feature but rather to the personal *style* with which the other embodies his characteristics and gives expression to his capacities and passions. None of these features of the other or the relationship need be seen as *necessitating* the lover's embrace of the beloved.

An initial choice to love might be birthed in a variety of ways. A young man walking down the street in thirteenth-century Florence might be captivated by the young woman he passes and might resolve in response to love her. Someone might awaken after an unexpected night with an old acquaintance to realize that he has become surprisingly dear, that she has become surprisingly vulnerable to him, and may proceed without further ado to open herself to him in love. A woman may come home after an evening she had imagined would lead nowhere to find that she can't help but replay and replay again her conversation with her date; captivated by him, she chooses him, commits to loving him. One may discover that one's affectionate bond with a friend of many years has been imperceptibly transformed into one marked by delight and desire—and one may deliberately and enthusiastically embrace the transformation. Or perhaps one sees a stranger across the proverbial crowded room, only to find that one's heart leaps inside. The range of possible narratives is effectively endless, of course, as is the range of goods to which one may respond when committing oneself to this kind of initial love. "A trivial cause may determine the direction of intense love. . . . It may be determined by physical beauty, or by purely sexual desire. And yet it may be all that love can be."[6] And it may happen quickly, indeed, famously, at first sight, with the heart reaching out enthusiastically to offer itself.[7]

This kind of rapid and impulsive movement of the heart will obviously leave room for surprises. But—and surely this is one of the great challenges and delights of love—the alert and sensitive lover will persistently be surprised, even after years of engagement with the beloved. "Is it possible, finally," Toru asks in Haruki Murakami's *The Wind-Up Bird Chronicle*, "for one human being to achieve perfect understanding of another?" Toru observes:

> We can invest enormous time and energy in serious efforts to know another person, but in the end, how close are we able to come to that person's essence? We convince ourselves that we know the other person well, but do we really know anything important about anyone?

Reflecting on his relationship with his wife, Kumiko, he muses:

> I might be standing in the entrance of something big, and inside lay a world that belonged to Kumiko alone, a vast world that I had never known. I saw it as a big, dark room. I was standing there holding a cigarette lighter, its tiny flame showing me only the smallest part of the room.[8]

On the basis of what she already knows, of course, the lover may opt to welcome the beloved into her heart on the basis of a stable, pre-existing disposition to find particular personality characteristics or physical features attractive. On the other hand, it is also not uncommon for features of another we hadn't expected to find attractive become so just because they are *the other's*: we bond with another, and then find his or her particular characteristics appealing. It is almost always a mistake to begin with an abstract, *a priori* set of desired traits, much less of putative deal-breakers, since the complex, messy circumstances of life and love can be expected to startle us repeatedly.

### C. The Character of the Initial Commitment

The initial commitment to loving another may be limited or open-ended (though the more limited it is, the more difficult it will be to recognize as an instance of love). And while the lover's determination may issue in what we might recognize as commitment, the lover may be entirely unsure just what the contours of her resolution actually are. She may simply know that she has made her love a matter not primarily or exclusively of impulse but also of choice.

The role that commitment may play in love at this point will depend, of course, on what becomes of the relationship between the lover and the beloved. The initial love of one may be matched with relative simultaneity by the initial love of the other and, if so, the two may begin the business of crafting a *we*. But of course unruffled progress toward increasing closeness is hardly the only possible outcome. Other options may present themselves.

## III. Commitment Throughout Love's Trajectory

The lover wants to persist in loving the beloved because of his many specific excellences and the many specific excellences of the relationship between the two. Commitment enables the lover to continue experiencing these excellences. But commitment will also be significant in other specific ways at different points along love's trajectory. I begin by reflecting on how we move past aversion to commitment—a movement that might be expected to repeat itself multiple times as love develops—before attending to various ways in which commitment proves persistently relevant at successive moments in love's trajectory.

### A. Commitment and Fluctuating Feelings

When one's heart registers the values at play and so proposes the choice to love, one might commit oneself simply because the beloved seems so thoroughly desirable and one wants to immerse oneself in the experience of his desirable qualities. But one might also wish to solidify one's decision as a commitment because one is very much aware of the fickleness of hearts, including one's own. One trusts the heart's response.[9] But one may also be aware that multiple factors might impede the heart's future responsiveness. Love in the relevant sense is not, of course, a feeling. But feelings signal and sustain the lover's orientation on the beloved, and their absence can prompt the lover to believe that something has changed, that the relationship is no longer worth her self-investment.[10] Since "any lover loathes the thought that she may 'happily' cease to love,"[11] a lover who is aware of the fickleness of hearts might seek prophylactically to safeguard her love against corrosion by anchoring it not merely in her moment-by-moment responsiveness to the beloved but in a commitment that changes her normative situation and which she cannot, therefore, ignore simply because her feelings change.[12]

The lover plagued by doubt or ennui may be aware that the beloved remains *valuable*, while wondering how she should continue to *respond* to the value she knows is there. She cannot reasonably take illusory comfort in the supposition that the beloved is objectively the best person for her, since, apart from her personal hierarchy of values, there is no objectively best person for her. If the beloved is to occupy a central place in her life, this will need to be precisely in virtue of her *commitment* to giving him priority.

She will have various resources at her disposal as she seeks to adhere to this commitment and to resist the temptation to detach. She can remind herself, for instance, that a choice to love worth making when she feels a certain way would also be worth making when she doesn't feel that way. That's because her feelings are best seen as *pointers* to the reality of the beloved's qualities, the nature of the relationship between the lover and the beloved, and the irreplaceable quiddity of the beloved, and these can continue to be the same whether, at a particular point, she *senses* them or not. And the knowledge that she's made a commitment can help to keep her focused on the developing relationship rather than on her changing moods.

Fears and limiting beliefs—which drive many aversive feelings—don't imply any actual lack of desirability on the part of the beloved. The things that matter with respect to the lover's love for the beloved—his inherent qualities, his capacity for love for and engagement with the lover, what the beloved could offer the lover as a partner, what the lover has already offered and what she intends to offer the beloved—all remain unchanged despite fluctuations in feeling.

Moods that might encourage the lover to abandon the beloved could include anything from boredom to responsiveness to the charms of another potential lover to the feelings of aversion that are predictable consequences of becoming intimately connected with and vulnerable to another.

- One may feel fear—as, for instance, of abandonment—which may prompt one to look for reasons to pull away.

- One may doubt that one *deserves* genuine care and affection.
- One may doubt one's own capacity to nourish and support the other reliably.
- One may experience deep-seated anxiety precisely at experiencing joy, pleasure, and ecstatic delight in response to the beloved—perhaps because one has been taught that one is not *worthy* of these things, that one will lose them if one embraces them, that one will be *punished* if one enjoys oneself, or perhaps because one has somehow imbibed the idea that they are morally or spiritually dangerous.
- One may nourish the gnawing worry that there might be a better alternative elsewhere.
- One may recoil at the beloved's failure to reciprocate one's delight and desire (something that may, of course, occur at multiple points throughout love's trajectory) and abandon him self-protectively or as a matter of pride.[13]
- One may find oneself exaggerating the significance of the other's imperfections.
- One may fear being engulfed or overpowered as one was by a domineering parent—we so readily cast our lovers in roles first played by our early caregivers—and search frantically for reasons to flee.

Regrettably, instinctive negative reactions of this sort frequently present themselves as more significant and terrifying than they actually are. There have unfortunately been recent attempts to normalize these irrational responses as instances of "Sudden Repulsion Syndrome." But, whatever the label one employs for them, there is good reason not to take them seriously.[14]

Avoiding negative feelings is no reason for the lover to abandon her commitment to the beloved, even during those periods when their *we* is dormant or nonexistent (perhaps because it has yet to come into being). And it is unreasonable to act on feelings of aversion when they fail to signal an actual risk to an actual good. Positive feelings may decline as a result of habituation. Negative ones may arise as a result of fears and limiting beliefs. And the prospect of a new romantic high may lead the lover to ignore, deny, or underestimate the lover's delights.

To give up—whether to pursue one or more other lovers or simply to avoid negative feelings—is to risk becoming a person blown hither and yon by shifting moods, to miss out on valuable opportunities with the beloved, and to embrace the mistaken assumption that experiencing great feelings is a test or measure of love (and so to make disappointment more likely). Maintaining commitment at times when feelings run dry or negative attitudes predominate helps the lover to develop the habits of loyalty and persistence in the face of adversity, habits that can be nourished only by being actively exercised. By contrast, the lover would acquire contrary, undesirable habits by giving up and starting over. To become the kind of person who runs off in search of good feelings rather than addressing the underlying issues giving rise to aversive reactions, especially when they reflect limiting beliefs and similar interior constraints, is to behave in ways with long-term negative consequences for any relationship. It will thus make sense to discount feelings of boredom or aversion and to focus on the beloved's delightfulness and desirability, whether one apprehends them by means of conscious sensory signals or not.

And of course the lover is not condemned necessarily to experience boredom or aversion indefinitely. Indeed, commitment on the part of the lover can also deepen her feelings—by directly releasing emotional blocks, by leading to heightened identification with the beloved, and by leading to continued shared experience, itself a source of deepened feeling.[15]

Committing oneself to being with someone after, if necessary, considerable difficulty is a matter of trusting one's initial vision of the beloved as delightful and desirable,[16] a vision that may readily be obscured in multiple ways. In the course of deciding whether to commit at various stages of a love-relationship's development, and in seeking to keep one's commitments one will, of course, encounter many barriers—difficulties, aversions, challenges of various sorts. But, as psychotherapist Judith Sills observes,

> [y]ou only have to tolerate the flaws you find in your lover a little bit more or back off a little bit less. Your partner and courtship itself will get you over the rest of the hump. It seems impossible that someone you are so critical of today could be someone you love deeply tomorrow. It seems impossible, but it happens all the time—if you let it. Your faultfinding, your doubts, your wavering interest are all a normal part of working your way toward commitment.[17]

Sills emphasizes: "Every time you notice a difference between what you wanted in a partner and what you've got, ask yourself this question: Can I live with it? Then, bend over backward in the direction of living with it."[18] As she stresses: "In order to be giving when you love, you have to let go of the critical, judgmental part of yourself."[19] To be sure, "a lot of changing has to be done in order to develop an intimate bond. But most of us put our efforts into changing our partners. The smart place to put your energy is in changing yourself."[20] "Your task," as Rumi puts it "is not to seek for love, but merely to seek and find all the barriers within yourself that you have built against it."[21] It has been increasingly common for people to focus on negative characteristics—to identify so-called "deal-breakers" and rule out many possible partners accordingly. Though Sills does not use this language, she is, in effect, suggesting that one focus, instead, on "deal-clinchers" or "deal-makers." Why might one proceed as Sills and Rumi imagine when making a commitment?

Doing this might be reasonable for the lover to do because (*i*) she has already opened herself to the beloved in virtue of the fact that he is positively delightful. Giving delight greater weight than, say, "compatibility" is reasonable because how the lover weighs real human goods is up to her (given that other requirements of practical reasonableness are satisfied). The various aspects of the beloved's delightfulness are genuine human goods. The lover can perfectly well value the beloved's presence in the world, or in her own life, over some tangible benefit or other, acknowledging that the beloved's delightfulness does, indeed, enrich her life. Having opened herself in delight at the beloved, when the lover encounters an unattractive feature of one kind or another, she has *already* come to value the beloved, to cherish him, to love him, and because she wants both to participate in a valuable relationship with him and simply to avoid experiencing stress that will reduce her ability to enjoy this relationship. The lover might, of course, simply experience strong positive subjective reactions to the beloved that she wishes to affirm and extend. But it might also be that she has also already made *commitments* that give the relationship a high priority or rule out treating the perceived negative features as determinative.

The lover might also proceed in this way because (*ii*) he recognizes that the putative negatives are trivial—worth treating as unimportant or as non-existent, even if they don't *feel* that way. He might, for instance, acknowledge that his own psychic pathologies can be counted on to prompt the exaggeration of negative features, while preparing himself to discount the instincts to which these pathologies give rise.

Of course, the lover might choose to avoid treating the negatives as decisive simply because (*iii*) she values the beloved and wants to *give* to him. And she might see this option as especially significant in light of the Principle of Fairness, since she might well prefer that the beloved view her own flaws and imperfections in the same way.

A further reason for the lover to treat the negatives as non-dispositive might be the recognition that (*iv*) even if the negatives are real, everyone has them, so that (*a*) he won't find a partner without some set of negatives (he might recognize that any contrary expectations should be treated as unrealistic and self-sabotaging); (*b*) abandoning the beloved will mean starting over and going through the same process again; and (*c*) leaving this partner will mean choosing habits of criticism and rejection that will undermine other relationships in the future.

The lover may note as well that he need not view putative incompatibilities as negative because (*v*) compatibility doesn't determine whether people can enjoy a thriving relationship,[22] and is best seen as an *achievement of* love rather than a *precondition for* love. (And compatibility in the sense of shared interests or beliefs can hardly be a stable basis for a relationship, since these change on an ongoing basis.)[23] Indeed, differences may be positive: it will be important to recognize that (*vi*) difference can be a source of provocation, intrigue, learning, and growth. And the lover may also proceed as Sills and Rumi suggest because he acknowledges that (*vii*) it is important to remember that (*a*) his partner isn't "wrong"—there is no such thing as a (or the) "wrong" partner, apart from one who is deliberately trying to cheat or steal from him or otherwise injure him—a sociopath, and (*b*) no actual or potential partner can fail to be good enough except with respect to the lover's own commitments and settled preferences, and he may already, as I have noted, have given high priority either to the beloved in particular or, more generally, to particular partners with her characteristics. And this means, in turn, that he needn't regard himself as under any obligation of morality or rationality to pursue a putatively superior potential alternative partner, nor should he regard himself as having cheated himself for having caused himself to miss out on such an imagined partner. In general, apart from specific commitments and, within the constraints of those commitments, stable preferences that give priority to partners with particular characteristics, there won't *be* better and worse partners (other than sociopaths). When one's heart goes out to a particular potential beloved and, in light of this, one commits to loving her, that *sets* the relevant priorities.

Commitment may prove a valuable response to inner fluctuations, conflicts, or disconnections at any of several stages of a relationship's development. The lover will, of course, be aware that the inner resistance she experiences may reflect not only concerns about the beloved's actual imperfections, which will obviously obtain (all beloveds have them), but also the reality that love itself may prompt panic and resistance. Ambivalence—focused on the fear of intimacy, fear of betrayal and abuse, guilt, etc.—is a predictable element of the experience of intimate vulnerability. It is nothing to find deeply troubling.[24] Doubts and insecurities and aversions are persistent outgrowths of limiting beliefs and may often reasonably be recognized and discounted as such. Further, of course, they could be expected to reappear in other relationships. Whatever mechanism might be used to deal with them there could be used to deal with them where the lover's responsiveness to the beloved is concerned. Some negative feelings will, of course, be rooted in actual tensions and conflicts. But, *en route* to commitment, these can often be resolved with understanding and forgiveness and respect.

## B. Commitment and Personal Growth

Commitment throughout multiple stages of love's trajectory is a way of developing and expressing admirable traits of character. Valuing the beloved, the lover wants to do something good for and in relation to him. She wants him to value her as one who has done this for him. And she wants to value herself as one capable of devotion, achievement, and heroism. Commitment thus also provides the lover with the opportunity to learn patience, both for its own sake and because of the opportunity doing so provides to experience the goods connected with her relationship with the beloved. And exhibiting patience is also an occasion for proper pride on the part of the beloved. Further, given that it is virtuous and healthy to forgive and to be patient, to be loyal and compassionate, maintaining her commitment to the beloved can offer the beloved additional opportunities to develop and exhibit a range of moral excellences.

The lover can only experience the relational goods she wants to experience with the beloved, goods that come from long-term self-investment in a relationship with the beloved and long-term engagement with the beloved, by adhering to her commitment. Opting out would mean declining the benefits derived from persistence—the benefits associated with learning to stay and the benefits associated with a genuinely long-term relationship. Starting over with someone else would mean losing what the lover had already achieved with the beloved, while also developing a habit of giving up, starting from scratch, and beginning again to invest in understanding, building trust and connection, understanding the beloved's behavior and inner life, and so forth.

### C. *Commitment, Selfhood, and Identity*

Commitment enhances the lover's own life in other ways, too. Whether in the context of embracing the beloved as partially constitutive of her identity (*i*) *en route* to forming a *we*, (*ii*) in the course of actually forming a *we*, or (*iii*) during a period when the *we* has been shattered, her commitment to loving the beloved contributes significantly to the structure and direction and meaning of the lover's own life. And once this kind of commitment has been made, the lover has further reason to avoid *abandoning* the structure and direction and meaning commitment has already offered his or her life. Her commitment embraces an attachment to the beloved that adds meaning and purpose to her own life. No doubt other relationships and activities and achievements already offer the lover meaning and purpose, but love adds powerfully to the array of factors that do.

### D. *Commitment and the Evocation of Love and Trust*

At each stage of a relationship's development, the lover can help evoke the beloved's responsive love by reaching out to him and remaining present to him. If he is apprehensive, less-than-fully trusting, the lover can, by committing, make the first move and put herself in a position to nourish and nurture and embrace the beloved. In so doing, the lover enables the relationship to grow and helps to make the beloved feel safe as he opens up.

The beloved may doubt the lover in particular—wondering whether, in light of her past behavior, she can be trusted to be constant or respectful or sensitive. And the beloved may doubt lovers in general in light of past experiences of betrayal, abandonment, or painfully superficial engagement. When this is the case, the lover must demonstrate commitment not only in the course of persistently wooing the beloved but also precisely to assure the beloved that she in particular is trustworthy and that it is possible and reasonable to trust, to *believe in love*.[25]

## E.  *Commitment and Comparison*

The incommensurability of the various aspects of welfare that underlies the practice of commitment will be relevant at multiple points. For the lover will frequently be inclined to wonder whether someone else, real or imagined, is or could be preferable to the beloved—whether he should give up pursuing her, give up trying to win her back, give up remaining with her at a difficult time. He will be aware, of course, that in most cases he can know relatively little about the relevant characteristics of any other potential beloved, so that this sort of speculation is likely to be an exercise in fruitless and unnecessarily distracting fantasy. More than this, however, as a general matter, the answer to the question whether someone else might be better will frequently be *no*.

This will be true because the various *kinds* of goods involved are incommensurable and because the various particular goods involved are incommensurable and non-fungible. The beloved is non-fungible with anyone else the lover might imagine wooing. The lover's relationship with the beloved is historically particular, and for this reason as well as its qualitative particularity non-fungible with any other alternative relationship. And the beloved's attractive qualities are distinctive, and so non-fungible with anyone else's. There are vastly many different ways to be witty, compassionate, beautiful, charming, courageous, loyal, and so forth. How the beloved, the lover's relationship with the beloved, and the various characteristics of the beloved and real or imagined alternative partners are to be *weighted* by the lover is not a matter of rational requirement: it is a matter of the priorities the lover has established by means of commitment.

These priorities need not involve sets of characteristics with reference to which the beloved and others are assessed. The lover may have made no previous firm commitments to giving priority to particular *characteristics* of potential lovers. Rather, the lover's commitments may simply give priority to the beloved *as an individual* over potential competitors or to the historically particular relationship between the lover and the beloved over other relationships. In any case, in virtue of the priorities established by her commitments, the lover will often have definitively ruled out ranking someone else as equivalent or superior to the beloved.[26]

## F. Commitment and Cost

It can in various ways be costly to woo the beloved, to work to reconnect with the beloved, to remain with the beloved despite conflict or illness or distance. Commitment enables the lover to measure the relevant costs.

Just how costly something *is* to the lover can only (assuming the other requirements of practical reasonableness have been met) be measured with reference to the lover's prior commitments. Suppose the lover has already committed to loving the beloved, to wooing him successfully and building a love-relationship with him. In this case, it cannot appropriately be objected to the lover's waiting for the beloved or working to woo him or working to regain his love or loyalty or persisting in her relationship with him through a difficult time that this is unreasonable because some other option would prove *less costly*.[27] Apart from the priorities established by the lover's commitments, there is no rational, objective basis on which to compare the various goods involved in a relationship with the beloved with those involved in a relationship with someone else. A future in which the lover waited for the beloved and won his heart would simply feature *different* goods from a future in which the lover opted for someone else. But there would be no way to compare these goods objectively apart from the lover's commitments. The lover *could not* choose one future over the other on the basis that either was overall better than the other.[28]

This is true not only because of the incommensurability of the various goods involved but also because the lover's future with the beloved is inaccessible to the lover—as is, of course, a future with anyone else. If people have free will, the future is, in principle, indeterminate, and for this reason unknowable.[29] Whether they do or not, the lover lacks the knowledge needed to project the content of a relationship with the beloved or with anyone else. She cannot know how long a relationship with the beloved would last versus how long a relationship with someone else would last, how the beloved would behave versus how someone else would behave, what goods might be realized with this or that potential partner, or anything similar. She has no justification either for *underestimating* the likelihood that she will succeed in wooing or reconnecting with the beloved *or* for *overestimating* the likelihood that desirable others will respond to her overtures.

Suppose, indeed, that, *per impossibile*, the lover did know that he could be with someone else longer than he would be with the beloved after successfully wooing her or reconnecting with her or remaining with her in the face of distance or conflict or illness. This would not make his decision to pursue the beloved unreasonable. This is so, again, in virtue of the incommensurability of the various goods involved. A certain amount of time spent with the beloved, time in which the lover can participate in the incommensurable, non-fungible goods offered and embodied by the beloved, is not worth objectively less than a larger span of time spent with someone else, no matter what goods the other person offers or embodies. This is because the relevant goods aren't generic: they're distinctive, specific to the different people involved. Thus, opting for the beloved over someone else in such a case would not be simply a matter of the lover's gritting his teeth and trying to exhibit integrity—but rather a matter of deeply loving the beloved and relishing the unique, irreplaceable goods that she offers and the unique, irreplaceable good that she *is*.

In attempting to think about the costs of embracing the beloved, the lover cannot reasonably contrast a worst-case scenario involving the beloved with a best-case scenario involving some real or imagined other, tempting as it may be to do this when things aren't going well. Rather, the lover cannot but recognize that it is *not* the case that she is beginning a *de novo* relationship with the beloved, or that others are ready to commit to her, or that, in the wake of a breakup, the beloved will unavoidably prove immovable, or that relationships with other potential partners will be stress-free.

As she contemplates an uncertain future, the lover need not expect to feel dull disappointment as she unhappily adheres to a commitment. Her preferences will be reshaped in virtue of her being committed to the beloved and in virtue of her experiences of closeness to the beloved. The experience of commitment can be expected to alter her responses over time. In addition, she will have reason to avoid making a habit of giving in to the desire for immediate gratification and so reducing her ability to participate in valued goods over the long-term.

The lover might regret not being sexual during a period without the beloved, or not participating in romantic drama with someone else, or not experiencing the pleasures of partnership. But the goods involved here would not and could not objectively outweigh the goods involved in being with the beloved—they are qualitatively different, and they could be weighed against each other only in terms of the lover's prior commitments. And, of course, even during this period, the lover might be reaping significant emotional satisfactions from engaging with the beloved, deepening her connection with him, given that progress toward establishing or reestablishing a *we* was occurring. And, in any case, the developing connection between lover and beloved would be inherently valuable whether or not consciously registered in the lover's emotional reactions—irreplaceably valuable and thus worth nourishing and sustaining despite difficulties.

Of course the lover could have made different choices. But the point is that love *is* a willing embrace of the other. And the lover has, *ex hypothesi*, chosen the beloved. It will never be the case that one person will be objectively better than all the others on all measures, though, of course, in light of the lover's own commitments, the beloved will enjoy a distinctive priority. But what's really decisive is that the lover is attached to the beloved and, especially, that the lover has *chosen* the beloved, committed herself to loving him and to wooing him successfully. Given the incommensurable goods made possible by different relationships, love will always finally be an embrace of the other in the face of alternatives. And this is true even though relevant prior preferences and commitments, if there are any, may rule out many options.

## IV. Commitment and Romantic Pursuit

Love's trajectory begins with the lover's choice of the beloved, a choice which may, though it need not, be transformed into a commitment. But this choice may meet varied responses. The lover's initial love for the beloved may elicit an ambivalent or even a negative response when it is first evident. Perhaps the lover is clumsy or in some way fails to evince characteristics that match those that form the beloved's love-map. Perhaps the lover is too intense, in a way that prompts the beloved to wonder, "Will I simply be overwhelmed?" Perhaps the lover's desire is so great that the beloved questions whether she could possibly merit it—or sustain it once the flush of initial passionate enthusiasm has dissipated. Perhaps the lover seems pathetically needy in a way that undermines her attractiveness. Or perhaps the beloved worries that responding positively to the lover's desire will result in a stultifying loss of freedom. Whatever the reason, the beloved responds hesitantly, or simply declines to engage as the lover desires.

### A. Embracing Commitment

Confronting resistance or rejection, the lover, feeling helpless and dejected, may simply bow out. A passive, fatalistic stance, rooted in doubts about personal efficacy, may strike her as natural and instinctive. But a lover who has actually committed to loving the beloved may seek, in light of her commitment, to woo him.

While our culture is full of narratives of successful romantic pursuit in the face of seemingly impenetrable resistance, it hardly needs to be said that the sort of commitment I envision here can find expression in a wide range of inept or even deeply counterproductive choices. The lover may think that she must only protest her love with sufficient volume and enthusiasm. She may be entirely inattentive to the deep-seated needs for understanding and intimate connection that underlie the superficial differences among people's romantic responses. She may prove entirely unable to give the beloved space, choosing instead to overwhelm him with a level of attention that finally proves not flattering but off-putting and that creates no opportunity for him ever to miss her. She may confuse techniques designed to attract a stranger into agreeing to go on a first date or engaging in a casual fling with the developed skills needed to build a genuine intimate bond. She may even engage so intensely that the beloved is left feeling threatened in some way.

There are, however, much more sensitive, respectful things the lover committed to wooing the beloved can do. She need not make the sorts of fumbles that have complicated romantic pursuits carried on by others too narcissistic to look beyond what makes them feel good to what might actually deepen their connections with those they desire. And, in the course of a genuinely intelligent romantic pursuit,[30] commitment can play multiple roles.

## B. Commitment and Persistence

The most fundamental is in ensuring persistence and determination. The desire for instant gratification will frequently seem overwhelming. And the tendency simply to mirror what the lover takes—rightly or wrongly—to be the beloved's own emotional state may have a debilitating role, since there will be the instinctive desire to match rejection with rejection.[31] A commitment to pursuing the beloved (respectfully and skillfully) will safeguard the lover against the temptation to give in to these impulses. He will recognize that emotional reactions come and go, and he may sometimes experience the romantic equivalent of the Dark Night of the Soul;[32] however, a commitment to realizing the particular goods made possible by a love-relationship with the beloved will equip him to keep those goods in view. Taking seriously the new normative situation he has created for himself by committing to wooing the beloved can safeguard him against being blown off course by his fluctuating feelings. "The faithful romantic lover waits, let us say, for fifteen years," one of Kierkegaard's pseudonyms muses.[33] Presumably the wait will not be as long for most people, but for those less patient than "[t]he faithful romantic lover," commitment will play a useful role in solidifying engagement with the other during what may sometimes prove to be an extended process.

## C. Reasons for Commitment

A prior commitment can be sufficient to justify the lover's willingness to wait and keep engaging. But a lover who has not already made such a commitment might choose to make one for multiple reasons: (*i*) the lover's delight in and desire for the beloved; (*ii*) the lover's attachment to the beloved; (*iii*) the lover's intent to offer the beloved a great gift: the gift of knowing her importance to the lover, knowing that the lover cares about and treasures her and so wants to give her the gifts that come from waiting for her and from being with her and accepting all of her unconditionally; and (*iv*) the opportunity that waiting for the beloved provides for the lover to experience the joy of determination and success. And of course these reasons might not only prompt an initial commitment to wooing the beloved but also provide ongoing support to adhering to such a commitment.

Having made a commitment to wooing the beloved, the lover need not *justify* waiting for the beloved to anyone, of course. In particular, it is not reasonable to ask how the relationship or the lover's commitment to realizing would fare *de novo*. It should not be compared with relationships with people to whom the lover is not already attached, to loving whom the lover is not already committed. Certainly, the lover has no intellectual or moral obligation to prove that the beloved would be the object of a *de novo* commitment.[34] And it would also be senseless to ask whether the lover would have desired to make the same commitment in view of developments occurring after the commitment, assuming these or comparable developments were not contemplated as reasons for altering or abandoning the commitment. Why stop there? Absent the improbable assumption that no later development would change the way the lover looks at the present, it would be arbitrary to make non-knowledge of the present at the time of an earlier commitment decisive, rather than non-knowledge of some other, later, set of circumstances (of which the lover is, of course, quite ignorant at the later time when she assesses the earlier commitment).

There is, of course, no (bizarre) obligation to avoid the difficult that would rule out waiting for the beloved or adhering to a commitment to wooing her through a difficult period. Such an obligation might be rooted in an imagined duty to maximize, but of course there could be no such duty given the incommensurability and non-fungibility of the various goods in question. There is certainly no duty to seek romantic satisfaction with as little delay as possible. People choose alternatives to romantic fulfillment all the time: consider someone's decision to opt for a financially based sexual relationship that is unlikely to become more intimate and committed, or Dante's love from a distance for Beatrice, or someone's love for a partner in prison or away at war. And of course there are many non-romantic choices that preclude romance—a choice to enter the priesthood or to focus on completing a demanding professional program or to invest deeply in one's work. Similarly, there is no way of saying that romantic connection with the beloved realized through patience, hard work, and personal growth should be seen as inferior in value to romantic connection with someone else gained more easily, even if it obtained for a longer period (and this is so even apart from the inherent instrumental and intrinsic value of the patience and hard work).[35]

A certain kind of naïveté might lead someone to imagine that initial romantic success or romantic reconnection ought to come easily if at all.[36] But there is no *a priori* reason to expect this, and human experience militates consistently against it. *Some* romances come easily, to be sure, and there is every reason to welcome ease of connection when it occurs, but there is no reason to regard romance as fruitless or undesirable in cases in which more effort is required. *Ex hypothesi*, the lover has determined, by making the relevant sort of commitment, that the beloved is worth significant, perhaps great, effort. And there will be great satisfaction in achieving the potentially difficult task the lover has set for himself, and substantial personal growth can occur in the course of powering through difficulty.

## V. Commitment and Romantic Reconnection

The same will be true, of course, when the lover seeks to reconnect with the beloved in the wake of a breakup.

Of course a lover who has neither committed to seeing a relationship through nor invested in any long-term way in the future of the relationship may simply walk away after a breakup, inclined passively or resignedly to let things take their course. And even a lover who's made a somewhat indeterminate commitment to deepening the relationship may judge that it is unclear how to proceed constructively or that wooing the beloved back will simply take too much work. There is, of course, no objective measure of how much too much might be apart from one's commitments, and those commitments may set the bar very high or very low, as the case may be.

Sometimes, either in virtue of a commitment already made to connect deeply with the beloved, or in virtue of a call of the heart that prompts a *new* commitment to do so on the occasion of the breakup, the lover will opt to do what is necessary to reestablish the relationship (while also, surely, addressing and moving past the difficulties that prompted the breakup).[37] Doing so in light of a prior commitment to making the relationship work will give the relationship the kind of priority it needs for the lover's pursuit of reconnection to make sense. But making a *new* commitment is also perfectly reasonable in light of the value the lover places on the beloved and the relationship. This might, indeed, be something the lover *discovers* at the time of the breakup: she might only realize at this time how much the other has come to matter to her.

A new commitment to reconnecting, or the decision to implement an earlier commitment to being with the other by choosing in this instance to pursue reconnection, can make perfect sense whatever the lover's prior temporal or emotional investment in the relationship. The relationship may have persisted only for a brief period before the breakup, but the lover may have chosen to give it a high priority and so warrant her dedication to restoring it. The relationship may have been casual up until the breakup: perhaps the lover gave it a low priority until that point; but, again, she may find that she now discovers it has come to matter to her more than she had anticipated and that she now therefore intends to commit resolutely to restoring it.

Clearly, wooing someone presents a challenge. But wooing someone who has opened up to one only to turn away in anger or fear or boredom or disconnection or distaste is potentially even more challenging. The contrast between past warmth and intimacy and present disengagement can readily prompt both discouragement and resentment. If these negative emotions are not to dominate, then anchoring gentle and respectful efforts to reconnect in a commitment rather than simply in the ego's momentary moods will be crucial.

Again, in this case, as in establishing the relationship in the first place, commitment may matter not only because it is essential to maintain the lover's engagement with the beloved but also because it may help to encourage a positive response on the part of the beloved. This will be true, in particular, if the beloved's departure from the relationship reflected doubts about the lover's reliability, whether as a consequence of the lover's own behavior or as a result of fears rooted in past intimate connections. Simply demonstrating thoroughgoing trustworthiness (while relaxedly and confidently allowing the beloved needed space) can be reassuring and appealing in such a case.

There will also, of course, be other reasons the lover might commit to reconnecting with the beloved.[38] For instance: Connection is not simply random. We instinctively connect with people who can expand our worlds and offer us something of value. This means, in turn, that the lover and the beloved can offer each other sometimes uncomfortable opportunities to grow. And *this* means that reconnecting with the beloved is a way in which the lover can restart opportunities for this kind of growth.

In addition, of course, simply going through the challenging process of effecting reconnection can be a dramatic occasion for additional growth. Further, the lover can hardly plan on simply giving up and starting over repeatedly. Doing so would mean declining to develop needed habits of sensitivity and determination and failing to address the problems in herself or in her relational habits that led to the breakup in the first place. Her relationship with the beloved will have broken up for specific reasons. In seeking to understand these reasons, address them, grow past them, and reconnect, the lover meets an important challenge. By learning to make her relationship with the beloved work, the lover accomplishes something she will need to do under any circumstances—and why should she wait to start over with someone else when she has the history she does with the beloved, when she is attached as she is to the beloved? And if whatever caused the relationship with the beloved to fail isn't addressed, she must realize that she will simply have to confront the same problem again. Why should she not simply do the inner and outer work required to correct it now, thus benefiting not only the beloved and the relationship but also herself by undergoing the needed personal growth even as she restores a valued relationship?

## VI.  Commitment and the Developing *We*

Once the lover and the beloved have formed a *we*, then—presuming that no breakup (or set of breakups) occurs, or that, if it does, the two reconnect—they are now free to settle into a long-term relationship, perhaps into permanence. And here, of course, commitment will play additional roles.

In a flourishing relationship, the choice to be a secure, perhaps permanent, *we* will be embodied in interpersonal *promises*. And these promises, exemplified by traditional marriage vows—though of course the promises need not be made in the context of, nor need they serve to create, a civil or religious marriage—are the most visible supports for an intimate partnership. (Obviously, that they are does not mean that every partner has made or will want to make such promises.) But commitments in my sense can serve to reinforce and can help to sustain these promises (though again, of course, not every partner has made or will want to make these sorts of commitments).

The most obvious case in which this might be relevant is one in which a partner's serious incapacity prevents active engagement in the relationship. Take the particularly poignant case of a partner suffering from severe emotional or cognitive challenges. One might sometimes think in such a case that the ill partner was in no position to rely on promises of love. But the well partner might nonetheless continue to care for the ill partner out of a commitment that would obviously continue to carry weight even if promissory obligation didn't.[39]

Another reason commitment might be useful in the context of a developing or developed long-term relationship is that promises rarely bind in thoroughly rigorous fashion. Just what we intend by our promises is often unclear. I may not be entirely certain what, exactly, my partner and I have promised to do, and it may therefore be useful to augment a promise with a personal commitment.

If the beloved has (as so many of us have) been wounded in ways that affect her openness to love or in virtue of which love triggers fear, the lover, caring about the beloved—quite apart from any promises he has made to her, and, indeed, as an underlying reason for making them, and separate from his desire to be with the beloved and to have a stable identity—will want to give the beloved a sense of security and freedom, a sense that she is loved and cherished and empowered. And this will provide reasons for the lover both to offer promises to the beloved and to support those promises by making commitments.

## VII.  Commitment Is Vital to Love

Love isn't always easy. It can be tempting to abandon a commitment to love in the face of ambivalence and aversion and anxiety and habituation. But these responses are par for the course when vulnerability is evoked—and this means that, while they may seem linked specifically with the relationship in which the lover now finds herself, she will recognize that they are likely to reappear, even if in different form, in other relationships: their occurrence says little about the merits of her relationship with the beloved. They are likely to be transitory, and the challenges they pose can be resolved. Giving up on a commitment because of these feelings would represent a surrender to fickle moods, the loss of the valuable things offered by her relationship with the beloved, both to her and to the beloved, and doing so could be expected to create the potential for disappointment and failure by reinforcing the dubious belief that felt intensity is a test or measure of love and felt dismay or disconnection evidence that love isn't viable.

Staying committed is often a challenge; the same is frequently true of expressing commitment appropriately. Commitment can prove oppressive if the lover signals it in a way that implies that the lover and the beloved already form a *we* when they in fact do not. It can involve a kind of self-investment on the part of the lover that may, if the lover is not sensitive and self-aware, prompt pushy and demanding behavior (behavior that sends the unspoken but blunt message: "Look what I'm doing for you! Aren't you grateful?"). And it can dispose the lover to ignore the need to *dance* with the beloved, to engage in an ongoing dialectic of engagement and retreat that does not smother the beloved and that nourishes attraction rather than killing it. So, while commitment is vitally important, the lover needs to express it in a way that clearly signals that it does not come with strings attached, that it does not conceal demands and unwarranted expectations, and so forth.

Provided it is appropriately expressed, commitment can play a vital role at each stage in the development of a romantic relationship. Love is a great good, offering tremendous value to romantic partners. But it may also prove demanding, tapping as it does into insecurities, doubts, and fears of all kinds. If a love-relationship is to grow and deepen, commitment is essential. Commitment is an opportunity for growth in determination, patience, and heroic persistence. It helps to shape identity and enlarge the self. It offers love security in the face of changes in mood. It helps to evoke love and trust. It provides the metric that enables the lover to know what is and is not too costly with respect to love and to see why comparisons between the beloved and others may be inapposite. Commitment can be valuable in the course of wooing the beloved or seeking to win back the beloved—it can serve effectively to balance the loneliness and lack of short-term emotional fulfillment the lover may feel in such cases. And, as a relationship solidifies, love can provide essential security to the lover and the beloved alike in the context of an ongoing partnership.

## Notes

1 This chapter represents a detailed elaboration of the discussion of the role of commitment in love offered in GARY CHARTIER, PUBLIC PRACTICE, PRIVATE LAW: AN ESSAY ON LOVE, MARRIAGE, AND THE STATE 41–48 (2016). For a more general explication and defense of the model of love I advance here, *see id.* at 8–100. I have in no case purposefully replicated my words from the earlier book, and I've written Chapter 5 of this book, as it were, "from scratch." However, I've drawn on some of the same notes that informed my earlier discussion of love, and my having done so may have led on occasion to similarities or overlaps in phrasing.
2 *Cf.* ROBERT NOZICK, *Love's Bond, in* THE EXAMINED LIFE: PHILOSOPHICAL MEDITATIONS 68 (1989); ROBERT C. SOLOMON, ABOUT LOVE: REINVENTING ROMANCE FOR OUR TIME 76–81 (1988).
3 I use different gendered pronouns at different points in this chapter to talk about the lover and the beloved. I vary the pronouns at different points in order, as much as reasonably possible, to avoid presupposing or reinforcing assumptions about the role of gender in love. But I use a different pronoun for each member of the pair with which I'm concerned simply as a matter of convenience: I have no desire to limit my focus to different-sex couples or to reinforce the illusion that such couples are the only ones that matter.
4 *See* SOLOMON, *supra* note 2, at 78.
5 The word "attachment" is used in a variety of ways in this context. Sometimes, attachment is understood as a stance in relation to the beloved marked by the lover's will to control the beloved in one way or another, often in order to manage his own vulnerability to her. This kind of lack of respect for the beloved's individuality represents a failure of love. Similarly, "attachment" may be used

to refer to excessive self-investment in particular events or occurrences within the context of a developing relationship. This kind of misplaced focus is, at best, counterproductive. My concern here is with attachment understood to be the healthy integration of the beloved into the lover's own self. Psychiatrist and psychoanalyst John Bowlby is the principal source of contemporary insight into the positive role of attachment in human development. *See* JOHN BOWLBY, 1 ATTACHMENT AND LOSS: ATTACHMENT (2d ed. 1999); 2 ATTACHMENT AND LOSS: SEPARATION: ANXIETY AND ANGER (1973); 3 ATTACHMENT AND LOSS: LOSS: SADNESS AND DEPRESSION (1980); A SECURE BASE: PARENT-CHILD ATTACHMENT AND HEALTHY HUMAN DEVELOPMENT (1988). A recent popular discussion of attachment: AMIR LEVINE & RACHEL HELLER, ATTACHED: THE NEW SCIENCE OF ADULT ATTACHMENT AND HOW IT CAN HELP YOU FIND—AND KEEP—LOVE (2010). *Cf.* WILLARD GAYLIN, REDISCOVERING LOVE 83 (1986).

6  2 JOHN MCTAGGART & ELLIS MCTAGGART, THE NATURE OF EXISTENCE 152 (1927). *Cf.* HELEN HARRIS, *Rethinking Heterosexual Relationships in Polynesia: A Case Study of Mangaia, Cook Island, in* ROMANTIC PASSION: A UNIVERSAL EXPERIENCE? 95, 121–22 (William Jankowiak ed., 1995).

7  *Cf.* HUGH PRATHER & GAYLE PRATHER, A BOOK FOR COUPLES 5–9 (1988); HUGH PRATHER, LOVE AND COURAGE 17–18 (2001). The other will *always* be a surprise, both because (*i*) she or he is always growing and because (*ii*) one's perspective on her or him is consistently limited. It is important to recognize, in addition, that it is skill in respecting, understanding, and caring for the other, rather than initial compatibility in interest or attitude, that is decisive for relational success.

8  Thanks to Clay Andrews for calling my attention to Murakami's treatment of this issue.

9  *See* bell hooks, *A Chat with the Author of "All About Love: New Visions,"* CNN, Feb. 17, 2000, www.cnn.com/chat/transcripts/2000/2/hooks/index.html (last visited Mar. 26, 2017) ("A major part of love is commitment. If we are committed to someone, if I'm committed to loving you, then it's not possible for me to 'fall out of love.'").

10  While feelings don't constitute love, and one can love in their regrettable absence, feelings help to support love; so it's good to know that it is possible to evoke deeper feelings in multiple ways. These include a meditative focus on reasons for the lover's gratitude for the beloved; active self-disclosure and emotional vulnerability; gentle touch; sex; experiencing variety together and engaging in novel and exciting activities together; humor; granting and experiencing space; dismissal of distractions; elimination of psychic factors that prompt disconnection; and proactive creation of cognitive dissonance, which will be resolved by the emergence of positive feelings. Most of these strategies are helpfully elaborated by anthropologist Helen Fisher. *See* HELEN E. FISHER, WHY WE LOVE: THE NATURE AND CHEMISTRY OF ROMANTIC LOVE 192–208 (2004).

11  STEPHEN R. L. CLARK, A PARLIAMENT OF SOULS 121 (1990).

12  Margaret Farley makes this same point with a focus on promising; *see* MARGARET A. FARLEY, PERSONAL COMMITMENTS 33–37 (1986); *cf.* JOSEPH RAZ, THE MORALITY OF FREEDOM 353–55, 385–89.

13  *See* THOMAS W. MCKNIGHT & ROBERT H. PHILLIPS, HOW TO WIN THE LOVE YOU WANT 267 (1998).

14  *See* Karley Sciortino, *Breathless: There's a Name for My Problem and It's Called Sudden Repulsion Syndrome,* VOGUE, Nov. 15, 2015, http://www.vogue.com/article/breathless-karley-sciortino (last visited May 7, 2017). Thanks to Tanja

M. Laden for calling this article to my attention. *Cf.* Hugh Prather & Gayle Prather, I Will Never Leave You: How Couples Can Achieve the Power of Lasting Love 128–29, 134–36 (1996) (discussing the same phenomena in connection with different stages of a relationship's development, referring to it in the first instance as "reversed infatuation"); Judith Sills, A Fine Romance: The Passage of Courtship from Meeting to Marriage 156–60 (1987).

15 *See* Barbara De Angelis, Passion 15–17, 53–54 (1998); Shmuley Boteach, Why Can't I Fall in Love? 194–95 (2001).

16 *See* Farley, *supra* note 12, at 48–49.

17 Sills, *supra* note 14, at 160.

18 *Id*. at 217.

19 *Id*. at 218.

20 *Id*.

21 *Rumi*, BBC Learning English, www.bbc.co.uk/worldservice/learningenglish/movingwords/quotefeature/rumi.shtml (last visited Mar. 21, 2017).

22 *See, e.g.*, Prather, Love, *supra* note 7, at 90, 92; Hugh Prather, Spiritual Notes to Myself 43 (1998); Prather & Prather, *supra* note 14, at 67–72, 127, 143–44, 164; Shmuley Boteach, Dating Secrets of the Ten Commandments 30–31 (2000); Linda Bloom & Charlie Bloom, 101 Things I Wish I Knew When I Got Married 90–92 (2004); John Gottman with Nan Silver, Why Marriages Succeed or Fail 23–24 (1994); John Gottman & Nan Silver, The Seven Principles for Making Marriage Work 129–55, 217–42 (1999); Harville Hendrix & Helen LaKelly Hunt, Making Marriage Simple: Ten Truths for Changing the Relationship You Have into the One You Want 24–36 (2013); Clay Andrews, *Breakup Excuse: We're Not Compatible*, Clay Andrews, Mar. 25, 2014, https://www.youtube.com/watch?v=SBZb7OU_zEw&t=228s (last visited Mar. 8, 2017). *Cf.* Henry Cloud & John Townsend, Boundaries in Marriage 162–64 (1999). The Prathers, in particular, emphasize the changing character of human egos.

23 *See* Criss Jami, Venus in Arms 2 (2012) ("To say that one waits a lifetime for his soulmate to come around is a paradox. People eventually get sick of waiting, take a chance on someone, and by the art of commitment become soulmates, which takes a lifetime to perfect.").

24 *See* John Armstrong, Conditions of Love: The Philosophy of Intimacy 130–34 (2002).

25 *See* Prather & Prather, Never, *supra* note 14, at 185; David Truman, *How to Create Deeper Love*, Soul Progress, www.soulprogress.com/html/Articles Folder/Articles/HowToCreateDeeperLove.shtml (last visited May 29, 2015).

26 In addition, by integrating the beloved into his identity, in at least a prospective *we*, the lover becomes attached to her in her narrative particularity. And no one else will, of course, bear just the same relationship to the lover's identity as the beloved does. Further, the lover not only commits to embracing the beloved with the particular characteristics she has but also comes increasingly to shape his responses in light of her particular characteristics, so that his desires come to focus not on the relevant characteristics in the abstract but rather on her own embodiment of those characteristics. *See* Nozick, *supra* note 2, at 68.

27 This might be imagined to be because the lover could, say, opt for someone else who would embrace participation in a *we* sooner or who would lack problematic characteristics that the beloved purportedly has.

28 In addition, the lover cannot realistically be expected to know anyone else's characteristics well enough to make the relevant comparison even if it were

objectively possible. This is so not least because anyone who lacked the beloved's problematic characteristics would have others. Further, given the openness of the future, it would be in principle uncertain which characteristics might manifest themselves, and how. And even if the future turned out to be metaphysically certain, it would remain, given the lover's unavoidable cognitive limitations, epistemically uncertain in ways that would rule out the needed kind of knowledge.

29   Events in the physical world are known to us through causal contact. A future free choice is, *per definitionem*, not there to be known in the present. But it's also not determined by present realities. So causal contact with present realities won't give one causal contact with it. And, assuming that retrocausation is impossible, neither the choice itself nor its effects will be in causal contact with one's perceptual faculties in the present, either.

30   Attempts to provide guidance for romantic pursuit are legion. They vary, of course, in sophistication, savoriness, and psychological acumen. Helen Fisher notes a variety of strategies that can prompt the emergence of romantic love: *see* FISHER, *supra* note 10, at 192–202. A classic introduction remains OVID, ARS AMATORIA (Julian May trans., 1930). There is a diverse array of contemporary popular discussions: *see, e.g.*, MCKNIGHT & PHILLIPS, *supra* note 13, at 1–273; LEIL LOWNDES, HOW TO MAKE ANYONE FALL IN LOVE WITH YOU (1996); LEIL LOWNDES, HOW TO CREATE CHEMISTRY WITH ANYONE (2013); DAVID J. LIEBERMAN, HOW TO GET ANYONE TO DO ANYTHING 1–30 (2000). Among more specifically gendered treatments of romantic or erotic pursuit, *see, e.g.*, ELLEN FEIN & SHERRIE SCHNEIDER, ALL THE RULES: TIME-TESTED SECRETS FOR CAPTURING THE HEART OF MR. RIGHT (2007); NEIL STRAUSS, THE GAME: INSIDE THE SECRET WORLD OF PICKUP ARTISTS (2008).

31   *See* MCKNIGHT & PHILLIPS, *supra* note 13, at 267.

32   *See id.* at 116–17.

33   SØREN KIERKEGAARD, *Æsthetic Validity of Marriage, in* 2 EITHER/OR 3, 70 (Walter Lowrie & Howard A. Johnson trans., 1972).

34   It is arguably meaningless to ask the question, since it concerns a subjunctive conditional having to do with a putatively free choice.

35   A relationship realized through patience, hard work, and personal growth might, of course, seem *more* valuable from the standpoint of many people; *cf.* MCKNIGHT & PHILLIPS, *supra* note 13, at 275–76 (focusing in this case specially on the restoration of a relationship after a breakup).

36   Someone I know once assured me that love ought to be as easy as falling off a log; this person has been married five times.

37   Again, of course, there is a substantial popular literature on the topic. For some thoughtful discussions, *see, e.g.*, BLASE HARRIS, HOW TO GET YOUR LOVER BACK (1989); CLAY ANDREWS, GET YOUR EX BACK: THE FOUR THINGS YOUR EX NEEDS YOU TO DO TO GET BACK TOGETHER (2014); CLAY ANDREWS, THE FIVE PHASES TO GET YOUR EX BACK: WHERE YOU ARE NOW AND WHERE YOU NEED TO GO TO GET YOUR EX BACK (2014); MCKNIGHT & PHILLIPS, *supra* note 13, at 275–314.

38   *See* HARRIS, *supra* note 37, at 6–9.

39   *Cf.* MARK C. MURPHY, NATURAL LAW AND PRACTICAL RATIONALITY 268 n.21 (1999) (seeming to view [what I am calling] a commitment, rather than or in addition to a promise, as germane in this kind of case).

# Conclusion
## Commitment and Flourishing

*Commitments help us realize our preferences, safeguard coherent identities and structures of choice, and participate extensively in the various aspects of well-being. But there are multiple reasons why we might sometimes sensibly adjust or abandon them.*

We make commitments expecting that we will be tempted to ignore or radically modify the plans they are intended to solidify and secure. If we supposed that we would fulfill our plans effortlessly, not encountering any inner resistance or else overmastering any such resistance without difficulty, we wouldn't bother committing. Commitments serve to keep us on track precisely when we want to change course. The question, then, is: *what sorts of reasons, if any, do they actually provide us for continuing to do what we've planned despite the impulse to do otherwise?*

In talking about what I'm calling a commitment, someone will sometimes say, "I made a promise to myself." This way of talking gets something right phenomenologically. A commitment is an undertaking *to do something,* an undertaking that gives one *a new reason* to do whatever it is one undertakes to do. And, if I fail to keep a commitment, I may feel the same sense of *shame* or *disappointment in myself* I'd feel were I to break a promise.

But, despite the phenomenological similarity, there seems to be a glaring difference. When I make a promise to you, I am conferring on you a moral claim on me, a claim that I do what I've promised. And, because that claim is yours, it's one you can ordinarily relinquish. Provided you are alive and *compos mentis,* you can release me from the obligation created by a promise I've made to you because my obligation is precisely an obligation *to you.*[1]

By contrast, of course, one can't simply release oneself from a commitment at will (as people often seem inclined to do with, say, New Year's resolutions). If one could, it wouldn't be a commitment at all in my sense, but only an *intention* or something similar. The point of a commitment is served only when, having made it, one *can't* release oneself from the obligation it creates just because one is inclined to do so. The idea of a promise to oneself captures the *feel* of a commitment, but not its underlying logic.

A promise obligates, on my view, because it is an invitation to trust and rely, and, often enough, because it either creates a relationship marked by a certain sort of expectation or dependence, because it serves an existing relationship of this sort, or both. To understand promissory obligation, we need to think about a promise in the context of this sort of relationship. But, while we may talk metaphorically about relationships with our future selves, both promising and committing make sense only on the assumption that we *are* our future selves—that they can't be viewed as other people to whom we assume trust-based obligations.[2]

We often treat commitments as creating new reasons for action, potentially decisive ones. But, if we understand things correctly when we reason this way, we need some alternative to thinking of commitments as promises to ourselves. Unsurprisingly, given the importance of commitments in our lives, there are several such alternatives. And there is no reason to see them as exclusive. Instead, they provide mutually reinforcing reasons to adhere to our commitments even when we want to abandon them.

In brief, it's unreasonable to abandon or modify a commitment at will because doing this will interfere with or reduce our ability to reach many of our goals—not only those we're currently pursuing but others as well. Doing so will undermine the coherence of our lives and the internal consistency of our choices. And doing so will deprive us of the opportunity to experience the full range and depth of human goods or to make rational plans for our lives.

Start with instrumental reasons. Assuming that we should accept some understanding of identity over time in virtue of which self-concern includes concern for ourselves in the future, then we have multiple strategic or instrumental reasons for *making* commitments. This means, first of all, that we have reasons to create conditions now that will increase the likelihood that we will behave in particular ways in the future. These may include forming habits, investing ourselves, devoting ourselves, in ways that shape our affective responses and channel our future energies. And they may also include creating sources of external incentives that will keep our efforts directed in the future toward the goals we've set in the present. This is all straightforward and non-mysterious: we have current preferences for ourselves in the future, and we anticipate that we will have various preferences in the future, and we choose accordingly.

But instrumental or strategic reasoning provides other forms of support for commitment-keeping as well. It's not just that we have *ex ante* reasons to act in ways that will causally influence our future choices but also that we have *ex post* instrumental reasons, having made commitments, to keep them. These reasons have to do with factors including the value of resolute commitment-keeping with regard to any and all projects, the signals commitment-keeping sends others, and the respect with which both we ourselves and others can be expected to respond to our adherence to our commitments. Keeping commitments supports many of our other activities, and our desire to engage successfully in these other activities gives us instrumental reason to keep individual commitments and to nourish the habit of commitment-keeping.

Instrumental justifications for commitment-keeping are independent of our ends, except, at any rate, for those ends that seem inescapable and don't depend on particular conceptions of what a flourishing life might look like. A fuller understanding of the human good will offer additional reasons to make commitments and to keep the ones we've made.

We might cluster a number of these together under the general heading of a concern for *coherence*. Here, the thought will be that self-integration, making an integrated story out of one's life, matters—that we have reason to want our lives to hang together and that, if we do, we will have reason not to ignore our commitments. This is so in part because a commitment serves simply to give one's life *focus* to one degree or another. If one wants a story that hangs together, one won't simply act as one happens to want to feel like acting from moment to moment. And, in turn, one will take one's commitments seriously, adhering to them unless one has appropriate reasons not to do so, because to disregard them will be to ignore or write off one's past and to create gaps between different segments of one's life. It may also turn one's life increasingly into a life of failure: through commitment, one has created reasons for action for oneself, and if one typically disregards them, one becomes, one marks oneself as, a person who simply doesn't, perhaps now can't, follow through.

In addition, some commitments are sufficiently self-involving, implicate our identities to such a degree, that abandoning them will mean letting go of ourselves and giving up on what gives meaning to our lives. We need to be careful about not disregarding moral constraints and the other aspects of human fulfillment that will persist in our lives even if we are forced to give up on these sorts of commitments. But there is good reason to make them, nonetheless; and, having made them, we will abandon them only on pain of something close to self-destruction. Obviously, many of the sorts of resolutions, plans, decisions that I've referred to here as commitments won't have this quality; they will likely be much more temporary, limited, and mundane. But concern about loss of identity will provide a significant reason to adhere to the subclass of commitments that really prove to be self-defining.

And of course the practice of making commitments itself *presupposes* that we will generally adhere to the commitments we make. Not only psychologically but logically, we act in a manner incoherent with the practice generally and with our individual commitments when we ignore those commitments without good reason.

Concern for our identities, for self-integration, is one kind of concern for the kind of well-being appropriate to creatures like ourselves. But, quite apart from this special case, there is an immense array of human goods, of aspects of well-being or flourishing or welfare or fulfillment. Acknowledging and responding to these goods provides further reasons for making and keeping commitments.

If our focus were just on our preferences, as when instrumental reasons for commitment-making and commitment-keeping are in view, then it wouldn't matter how we proceeded with respect to the objects of our choice, given that we achieved whatever our preferences happened to be. But if there are actual, preference-independent goods to be discovered and plumbed, then we will have reason to commit in order to test and explore their depths and embrace their richness and complexity. We will miss out, in short, if we stay on the surface. We need to dive deeply, at least sometimes, and this will mean planning for the future, investing over time, and so committing.

In addition, both short-term and long-term planning require priorities. Because the various aspects of well-being are incommensurable and non-fungible, there will be no guaranteed rational ordering of the goods we might realize at particular choice-points: we will simply have to *choose*. And while acting in accordance with our immediate preferences may sometimes be entirely reasonable, some sorts of planning require us to budget scarce resources and to use limited time in one way or another. When doing this, we need priorities that extend beyond the present moment. And because priority rankings aren't simply *given*, they need to be established—established by our commitments. But of course our commitments can serve this function only if we treat them *as* commitments, if we take them seriously and generally adhere to them.

Once a commitment is made, it will become easier to keep because keeping it will become a habit. Having made and kept it will shape one's preferences in such a way that keeping it will be an increasingly natural response to those preferences. In addition, one will thus feel good about the achievement of one's goals because of one's commitment to achieving them.

The particular goods in virtue of which one makes a commitment may be one's own; they may be others'; or they may be shared. Certainly, one may make a commitment very much in light of the positive consequences of fulfilling the commitment for one or more other. And one's concern for the other or other's one seeks to benefit by means of a commitment may be among the motives for adherence to the commitment. But suppose one is tempted to abandon the commitment precisely because of the benefit shifting one's focus might yield for beneficiaries other than the other or others in whose interest one made the commitment? In this case, noting that the original beneficiaries would be disadvantaged were one to move on from the commitment wouldn't suffice to justify continued fulfillment of the commitment, since opting for the tempting alternative would lead to real benefits for some of those affected by one's choice to pursue that alternative. For it to make sense for one to continue giving priority in the relevant way to the original intended beneficiary or beneficiaries, one's efforts must already have been focused *by a commitment*. A commitment must already have *selected* this other or these others as the focus of one's actions.

We have multiple reasons to make and keep commitments. And we have reason to take our commitments seriously: if we don't do so, they can't play the roles in our well-being that make them worthwhile in the first place. But of course there are multiple circumstances under which commitments may reasonably be revised or disregarded. We can't simply say, we have every reason not to want to say, that this will be a matter of making ungrounded situational judgments. Rather, the circumstances under which we may opt not to adhere to our commitments, or may, indeed, find ourselves obligated not to do so, can be identified in light of the nature of commitment and our reasons for making and keeping commitments generally.

The analogy with making and keeping promises will be instructive here.[3] We can't simply release ourselves from our commitments, as I've noted. In this respect, commitments are quite unlike promises. But other standard reasons for not keeping promises will obviously apply in the case of commitments. So, for instance, there is no point in attempting the impossible: if I commit to practicing in order to qualify for an Olympic basketball team, only to lose my arms in a freak accident, then, absent remarkable prostheses, I will simply be unable to play basketball, and so to practice. It's important to emphasize that impossibility is not the same thing as great difficulty, much less psychic resistance. Commitment may be designed precisely to get us past the hurdles posed by these sorts of challenges, and referring to the fulfillment of a commitment as impossible in the face of such challenges may frequently be a cop-out. But there will, obviously, be cases of genuine impossibility, and it would be foolish to persist in one's commitments in such cases.

Even in the absence of physical impossibility, adhering to a commitment may prove genuinely pointless. I may commit to performing a difficult mountain-climb in order to take pictures of a meteor shower, only to discover that an atmospheric disturbance will completely obscure the meteor shower. Climbing the mountain and taking the pictures remains physically possible in this case, but there is no point to fulfilling my commitment because I won't be able to achieve the goal the commitment was designed to serve. Sometimes, of course, the good I seek to realize when I make a commitment is a good that will be realized just by doing what I've committed to do. For instance, if I commit myself to being your friend, I'm not seeking to realize some other good to which the friendship is instrumental (if I am, then it's not clear I'm really committing to being a friend at all). And here, as long as you're alive and able to interact with me (and perhaps in some cases even if you're not) I am realizing the purpose of my commitment whenever I engage with you or further your well-being. But, where the purpose of a commitment is external to the commitment, the commitment may prove pointless if the purpose turns out to be unachievable, so that adhering to the commitment will be foolish.

Some factual or normative judgments will be integral presuppositions of our commitments. Perhaps I commit to behaving in a certain way because I believe it is admirably virtuous, for instance—not required but supererogatorily good. Or perhaps I commit to undertaking a demanding diet because I believe it will rid me of my diabetes. Or perhaps I commit to participating in a gaming session at a friend's house because I've given no thought to the possibility that a loved one I haven't seen for many years will be visiting at the same time. If the beliefs underlying these commitments (which, as the last example underscores, need not be conscious or explicit when the commitments are made) turn out to be false, then there will be no reason (so far as the examples themselves make clear) why I should adhere to them.

Among the sorts of assumptions that might ground our commitments are assumptions about our own capacities. Even with intense practice, for instance, it may be physically impossible for me to perform a task I've committed to performing, and if this is really so I can certainly at some point choose reasonably to admit defeat—even if I may also need to acknowledge that I was insufficiently attentive to my own body's limits when making the commitment. However, recognizing the possibility of this sort of limitation can sometimes be a too-easily-accepted rationalization for accepting failure. This is particularly so when the assumption one makes has to do with one's own psychic rather than physical capacities. One can move past emotional blocks in ways that one can't always move past physical ones; and, indeed, fortitude and determination amount precisely in many cases to surmounting one's own aversion and other sorts of emotional resistance. And believing that one is capable of achieving a goal is often a crucial precondition to doing so. The view that psychic limitations, in particular, are insurmountable seems likely to prove false in many cases; and that habit of taking this view seems likely consistently to impede performance.

And of course the fact that, in virtue of psychic resistance of one sort or another, I fail to keep a commitment at a particular moment does not mean that I am incapable of keeping the commitment generally or that I should abandon it. If I am committed, say, to not drinking alcohol for the next six months and I opt to take a drink, it doesn't follow that my reasons for not drinking during the relevant period no longer apply or that I am no longer capable of acting on them. I can still adhere to my commitment, regretting my lapse, rather than treating the commitment as an all-or-nothing matter that can simply be ignored after my mistake. To treat the commitment this way will ordinarily be to ignore both the reasons I had for making the commitment in the first place—the goods to be realized in and through the commitment—and the reasons I have for adhering to the commitment once made. These will continue to apply even after a moment of weakness.

Sometimes, of course, fulfilling a commitment would be morally wrong for one reason or another. Making and keeping commitments is a way of flourishing. But it is not, of course, the sole constituent of well-being. It will not be reasonable to ignore moral constraints on one's actions when determining whether to adhere to a commitment. The same underlying reasons that make ignoring commitments unreasonable also make ignoring other constraints on our choices, constraints related to our own well-being and the well-being of others, unreasonable as well. These underlying considerations make ignoring other moral constraints unreasonable even when, viewed *in abstracto*, a commitment might encourage us to disregard them. It may thus in particular be unreasonable to adhere to a commitment when doing so is inconsistent with interpersonal moral obligations, when doing so involves a purposeful or instrumental attack on one's own well-being, or when doing so is inconsistent with a commitment one has *already* made.[4]

Beyond this, of course, commitments will include their own built-in limitations. Commitments are not ordinarily made unconditionally. Some, as I have noted, may be made with an eye to surmounting emotional resistance; but others may assume, implicitly or explicitly (implicitly because we may simply be in the general habit of understanding our commitments this way), that strong aversion will be a perfectly good reason for not fulfilling particular plans. One can hardly make all commitments this way: doing so would undermine the point of making and keeping commitments. But many of the plans we commit to fulfilling simply aren't that important, and we may well treat them as such.

The important thing to recognize here is that, even if it's consciously framed this way, a commitment is rarely just to do this or to avoid doing that. A whole tissue of background assumptions and limitations and qualifications will frequently be built in to a given commitment. The commitment is thus not a commitment to do $X$, but a commitment to do $X$ under these circumstances, with those qualifications, on these assumptions. . . . And, assuming the commitment as one has actually made it doesn't rule out this or that justification for non-performance; one may bring these to the surface by asking, *If I'd thought about that when I made the commitment, would I have made the commitment anyway?*

We will need in such cases to take into account not only the point of a particular commitment but also the point of commitments more generally—first and foremost, in many cases, to help us achieve our goals despite temptation, aversion, sloth, boredom, and so forth. It will make no sense to view a commitment as typically or ordinarily worth abandoning in the face of these kinds of emotional responses, for in that case it would be unclear why it made sense to commit at all.

Understanding the inner structure of a commitment will also mean acknowledging the distinction between the real significance of the commitment and the various steps I've planned on taking to fulfill the commitment. One might allow oneself to vary the latter without in any way ignoring the importance of the former. So, for instance, when I began work on this book, I intended to write a certain number of words each day. My progress was interrupted when I was sick a few weeks ago. And distraction and tiredness—and, frankly, lack of ideas—slowed me down more recently. I deliberately chose, however, to complete today the amount of work I would normally have expected to complete in three days in order to make up for work I'd failed to complete earlier in the week. I allowed myself to be overwhelmingly tired yesterday without guilt while keeping this project on schedule by writing more today.

Recognizing the various limits on the commitments we make is not to deny, of course, that we can, obviously, make commitments in virtue of which it is *not* reasonable for us to change our minds. Commitments of this sort may prove thoroughly admirable, but they will also often be difficult to fulfill, especially if they involve long-term plans of one sort or another. And, of course, given that one shouldn't make commitments if one is too likely akratically to abandon them—both because one will in so doing miss out on the relevant goods, and perhaps also on goods one might have realized through some alternate commitment, but also because one may make it harder for oneself to keep commitments generally—one should be careful about committing to do physically or psychically difficult things. At the same time, such commitments can offer opportunities to realize goods that might not be achievable in other ways. In addition, defining oneself as a person who has made and kept challenging commitments can not only give one access to these goods but give oneself and others reason to view one with respect.

As I've noted, one reason to make commitments is to define one's identity, and one reason to keep one's commitments is that not doing so is a way of undermining one's identity. The connection between commitment and identity is also at least one source of the parallel between commitments and vocations. Both serve to give structure and direction to people's lives. And both provide a measure of *focus*: there are lots of goods, in principle, that might claim our attention, lots of goods we might seek to realize in our own lives and the lives of others. In different ways, commitments and vocations make particular goods *ours*. But commitments appear to be chosen, while vocations seem to be demands we confront.

The differences are less pronounced, however, than we might think. On the one hand, there may be few if any options for us when we confront the question whether to make commitments with regard to particular goods: our histories and circumstances and preferences and prior commitments may have narrowed our options considerably. And a vocation may present itself as an offer rather than a requirement. Some vocations will differ phenomenologically from some commitments, but the two can turn out to be quite similar. And if there are problems with singular requirements of the sort vocations may present themselves as being—if theistic voluntarism, consequentialism, and moral particularism are all unappealing—we might find ourselves concluding that what have seemed to be vocational demands are best understood, instead, as features of richly value-laden circumstances that compellingly evoke our loyalty and so prompt our commitment.

Interpersonal erotic love offers useful illustrations of the ways in which commitment can function to focus us on particular goods and help us realize those goods in our lives. (It would be similarly illustrative of the dynamics of vocation, I suspect.) Delight, desire, care, attachment—the evocative responses that (as I should be inclined to say) *propose* love to us are characteristically registered at the level of feeling. But, when I love, I embrace them, and embrace the other, as a matter of choice. This can, though it need not, be a matter of commitment. And commitment can continue to play out in the course of romantic pursuit, of the development of a relationship once pursuit has been successful, of reconnection if a breakup occurs, and of the solidification of a relationship into a permanent partnership. While interpersonal promises will play crucial roles at multiple junctures, commitments may parallel and support these promises, and they may prove to be essential to ensuring that a relationship has a future at difficult times.

The practice of making and keeping commitments helps to ensure that we flourish—that we experience fulfillment, well-being, welfare—in ways we couldn't without it. Commitments help us achieve our goals, whatever those goals might be. They help us to craft and maintain coherent identities. And they enable us to participate richly and deeply in particular varieties of human possibility that become distinctively our own precisely in virtue of our commitments. Commitments offer us structure and direction—yet not structure and direction imposed on us by arbitrary fiat from outside us, but structure and direction that flow from our own natures, characters, and choices. Commitments play a crucial role in self-cultivation and self-creation: we have every reason, judiciously, to make and keep them, and so to continue writing the stories of our own lives.

## Notes

1 This does not mean, of course, that there might not be *other* reasons, perhaps decisive reasons, to do something one has promised to do even if, in virtue of release by the promisee, one no longer has any specifically *promissory* obligation to do it. There might be persisting duties of *fairness*, for instance; and non-performance might be unreasonable as well in virtue of a commitment paralleling one's promise.
2 With characteristic acuity, Stephen Clark suggests (in personal communication) that I cannot simply release myself now from the commitment "I" made in the past at least in part precisely because the past "I" is not around to release me and that the idea of "a promise to myself" gets this feeling right. This may ultimately prove correct. But, if it does, and if a prior self thus isn't around to release me from a promissory obligation, this would make the idea that the obligation continued to obtain at least somewhat more doubtful. After all, if the self that received the promise isn't around to release me, it also seems to be the case that I'm not the self that *made* the promise; *that* self isn't around to *keep* it. I'd prefer a more robust conception of identity. I examine some related issues in *Contracts and Vows*, 5 Ox. J. Law & Rel. 482 (2016).
3 Some of the reasons I suggest might justify declining to keep a commitment parallel reasons characteristically offered for not adhering to promises or contracts; *see*, *e.g.*, Margaret A. Farley, Personal Commitments 67–109 (1986); Marvin A. Chirelstein, Concepts and Case Analysis in the Law of Contracts 62–79, 128–46 (3d ed. 1998); E. Allan Farnsworth, Changing Your Mind: The Law of Regretted Decisions 22–28 (1998).
4 *See* Mark C. Murphy, Natural Law and Practical Rationality 209–11 (1999).

# Index

# About the Author

**Gary Chartier** is Distinguished Professor of Law and Business Ethics and Associate Dean of the Tom and Vi Zapara School of Business at La Sierra University in Riverside, California. He is the author, editor, or co-editor of twelve other books, including *Public Practice, Private Law* (Cambridge, 2016), *Anarchy and Legal Order* (Cambridge, 2013), *Economic Justice and Natural Law* (Cambridge, 2009), and (with Chad Van Schoelandt) *The Routledge Handbook of Anarchy and Anarchist Thought* (Routledge, 2019). His byline has appeared over forty times in journals including the *Oxford Journal of Legal Studies*, *Legal Theory*, and *Law and Philosophy*. He is a member of the American Philosophical Association and the Alliance of the Libertarian Left and a senior fellow of the Center for a Stateless Society.

After qualifying for a BA in history and political science from La Sierra (1987, *magna cum laude*), he explored ethics, the philosophy of religion, theology, Christian origins, and political philosophy at the University of Cambridge, earning a PhD (1991) with a dissertation on the idea of friendship. He graduated with a JD (2001, Order of the Coif) from UCLA, where he studied legal philosophy and public law and received the Judge Jerry Pacht Memorial Award in Constitutional Law. The University of Cambridge presented him with an earned LLD in 2015 for his work in legal philosophy. A proud southern California native who wishes he had attended UC Sunnydale, he shares a slowly improving 1920 home in Riverside with Willow Rosenberg the Kitty. His hobbies include film; long-arc television; genre fiction; spicy food; politics; writing; human psychic and social dynamics; interminable conversation; and the esoteric, the quirky, and the arcane. His motto is E. M. Forster's "Only connect." Visit him online at www.gary chartier.net.

For Product Safety Concerns and Information please contact our EU
representative GPSR@taylorandfrancis.com Taylor & Francis Verlag GmbH,
Kaufingerstraße 24, 80331 München, Germany

Printed and bound by CPI Group (UK) Ltd, Croydon, CR0 4YY
11/04/2025
01843992-0002